AF564677

SECURITIES MARKET

OPERATION AND REFORMS

SECURITIES MARKET

OPERATION AND REFORMS

Edited by

BALWINDER SINGH

and

JASPAL SINGH

Faculty Members,
Department of Commerce and Business Management,
Guru Nanak Dev University, Amritsar

DEEP & DEEP PUBLICATIONS PVT. LTD.

F-159, Rajouri Garden, New Delhi-110027

SECURITIES MARKET
OPERATION AND REFORMS

ISBN 81-7629-724-0

Typeset by ASHISH TECHNOGRAPHICS,
3190, Mohindra Park, Shakur Basti, Delhi-110034.

Printed in India at ELEGANT PRINTERS,
A-38/2, Maya Puri, Phase-I, New Delhi-110064.

Published by DEEP & DEEP PUBLICATIONS PVT. LTD.,
F-159, Rajouri Garden, New Delhi-110027.
Phones: 25435369, 25440916
E-mail: ddpbooks@yahoo.co.in • deep98@del3.vsnl.net.in
Showroom:
2/13, Ansari Road, Daryaganj, New Delhi-110002 • Telefax: 23245122

Contents

Preface

The field of securities market in India has undergone series of changes since Liberalization in 1991. The literature related to the field has consistently grown, additional instruments have been introduced and majority of the concepts and theories too have undergone a sea change. The developing economies, all over the globe, always are prone to the threat of fallout from the external environment. Therefore, it becomes all the more important that they should try to develop a financial system that reveals perfect information and facilitates an efficient capital allocation with reduced transaction cost.

This book is based on thought provoking empirical research articles, relevant to the field, that help the reader to understand the subject better and to strengthen the fundamentals of the subject.

We sincerely are of the view point that the serious students pursuing research in the field would acquire balanced knowledge about the subject and it is surely going to stand in a good stead for those aiming for developing command over the latest developments in the field and would help them to explore the research areas beyond the given contents of the book.

This book has been designed to meet the requirements of academicians, students and research scholars in their pursuit in the area of commerce covering topics like IPOs, Mutual Funds, Derivatives, Investor Protection, ETFs, Dematerialization, Stock Market Efficiency and the like.

Amritsar

BALVINDER SINGH
JASPAL SINGH

List of Contributors

1. **Bawa Singh Goraya and Dinesh Kumar,** Lecturer, Govt. College, Ajnala, Distt. Amritsar and Lecturer, S.L. Bawa D.A.V. College, Batala, Distt. Gurdaspur, Punjab.
2. **Pawan Kumar Taneja and P.P. Singh**, Faculty Members, Punjab College of Technical Education, Ludhiana, Punjab.
3. **Dr. Sanjeev Sharma and Kapil Gupta**, Senior Lecturer (Selection Grade) and Lecturer, Post Graduate Deptt. of Commerce, Hindu College, Amritsar.
4. **Dr. M.C. Garg and Deepti Gakhar,** Chairman Deptt. of Commerce, Chaudhary Devi Lal University, Sirsa and Ph.D. Scholar Deptt. of Business Management, GJU, Hisar (Haryana).
5. **Dr. Mandeep Kaur and Renu Sharma,** Sr. Lecturer, mkaur02@yahoo.co.in and Research Fellow, renu_23resh@yahoo.co.in G.N.D. University, Amritsar.
6. **Rohit Saini,** Research Fellow, Punjab School of Economics, G.N.D. University, Amritsar.
7. **Dr. K.V.S.S. Narayana Rao,** Professor of Finance, S.P. Jain Institute of Management & Research, Mumbai, nrao@spjimr.ernet.in.
8. **Karamjeet Kaur,** Lecturer and Head, Post-graduate Department of Commerce, ASSM College, Mukandpur, Punjab-144507; e-mail: ksandhu-75@rediffmail.com.
9. **Dr. Subhash Chander and Manjinder Singh,** Professor, Deptt. of Commerce and Business Management, G.N.D. University, Amritsar. Lecturer, Deptt. of Commerce,

A.S.S.M. College, Mukandpur (Nawanshahar)-144514, Punjab.

10. **Mohit Gupta, Navdeep Aggarwal and S.K. Singla,** Faculty Members, Department of Business Management, PAU, Ludhiana (Punjab).

11. **Dr. Jaspal Singh and Poonam Sharma,** Sr. Lecturer and Research Fellow, Commerce & Business Management Deptt., G.N.D. University, Amritsar (Pb). E-mail: jassop@rediffmail.com

12. **Rekha Handa,** Lecturer-in-Business Management, Khalsa College for Women, Ludhiana.

13. **Dr. Balwinder Singh and Pooja Malhotra,** Reader and Research fellow, Department of Commerce and Business Management, G.N.D. University, Amritsar (Punjab).

14. **Dr. Sakshi Vasudeva,** Lecturer, Rai University, New Delhi.

15. **Balwinder Singh and Dr. R.K. Mittal,** Reader, Deptt. of Commerce and Business Management, G.N.D. University, Amritsar (Pb) email: bssssaini@yahoo.com and Professor and Head, Deptt. of Commerce, Kurukshetra University, Kurukshetra.

1

Awareness and Protection of Investors

An Empirical Study

BAWA SINGH GORAYA AND DINESH KUMAR

Capital market is the medium through which investment is allocated among alternative uses in a market economy. In such an economy, capital market is the investment planning office. It decides how many resources will be available for investment by firms throughout the economy; and at what cost.

From the early 1980s onwards, there has been a shift in India's economic policy regime, away from direct influences upon resource allocation by the State, towards a greater role for markets. One major plank of these reforms has been an attempt at developing financial markets as an alternative vehicle determining the allocation of capital in the economy. (Shah, 1998)

Reform of capital markets is critical to India's long-term development. Past reliance on government investment and bank lending has produced poor results. These practices clearly will not provide the amounts of resources necessary for rapid future growth, nor allocate them as efficiently as a capital market—the "planning office" for a market economy—

can. Government oversight is critical to developing an efficient stock market, by requiring disclosure of relevant financial information, limiting transactions costs for securities trading, and promoting transparency of market operation. (Fox, 1999) So the Government initiated reform of financial sector (including the securities market).

Since its creation, SEBI has sought to improve the structure and functioning of stock exchanges and to ensure disclosure and investor protection. But the process of opening the Indian capital market has been uneven. Abolition of the Comptroller of Capital Issues in 1991 (with residual responsibility for oversight of new issues given to the Securities and Exchange Board) led to large numbers of initial public offerings in 1992–94. The number of public companies rose dramatically from 1,000 in the late 1980s to 6,000 by 1994. The historical experience of investors, whereby an IPO was an almost automatic winner, created an acceptance in the marketplace for any new issue. The liberalization of the economy led to revaluation of stock prices, and investor enthusiasm produced a speculative bubble during 1992–94. Stock prices were bid up, and prices of many new issues rose to levels simply unjustified by future earnings prospects. Some highly questionable, or outright fraudulent, financial deals were sold to an unsuspecting public. Compounding those problems was a stock market system that lacked an adequate trading, processing, settlement, payment, and registration infrastructure. The result was a major stock market crash that thoroughly spooked retail investors (Fox, 1999) who are no doubt the most important player in the capital market.

Investors can be categorized as institutional investors, company management control groups and individual investors. Individual investors are at most disadvantageous position as they are not only scattered and unorganized, but posses limited authority and resources and relatively less knowledge of what is going in the company of which they are shareholders. Investors have a number of grievances relating both to primary market and secondary market, such as misleading advertisement, delay in dispatch of allotment letters/refund orders, delay in transfer of securities, price rigging, misleading disclosure in prospectus, insider trading, lack of transparency in transactions, low level of liquidity, etc.

Section one of our present paper examines the various measures taken for protection of investors and section two measures the awareness and effectiveness of these steps from investors' point of view. For this purpose, 250 respondents were chosen on the basis of convenient sampling. Despite best efforts, 150 filled questionnaires were collected from them. The collected data were analysed with the help of tables, percentages and arithmetic mean.

SECTION I

This sections deals with evolution of capital market in India and measures taken to promote and protect interest of Investors.

Capital market in India formally came into existence when The Bombay Stock Exchange was founded in 1875. It is the leading exchange in the country, and until recently accounted for about 80 percent of all stock transactions. Twenty-two other stock exchanges also operate in India, as the government has restricted the geographical reach of each of its exchanges. There are some 7,000 listed stocks, 7,000 brokers who are members of the 23 exchanges, along with an estimated 100,000 sub-brokers who interface with investors, a million active traders, and perhaps 20 million citizens who hold equities in some form, usually a mutual fund. Despite its long history and large number of listed stocks, the equity market has had major problems. The exchanges operated with high commissions, a lack of disclosure of actual transaction prices, serious paperwork problems, and unreliable clearing and settlement. The issue of new stocks was controlled by a government agency, the Comptroller of Capital Issues. With a mission to ensure the quality of new IPOs, the CCI reviewed the financial situation and prospects of the issuing company, and approved the price at which the new issue could be offered. Because of its conservative approach, new issues frequently were sharply under priced. (Fox, 1999) This lead to various malpractices in the capital market.

From late 1993 onwards, the Indian State embarked on

a radical reforms program which completely transformed market institutions. This program consisted of creating four new securities market institutions: the Securities and Exchanges Board of India (SEBI), the National Stock Exchange (NSE), the National Securities Clearing Corporation (NSCC) and the National Securities Depository Limited (NSDL) (Shah, 1998).

The Securities and Exchange Board of India

Established in 1992, SEBI has a dual mandate of regulating capital markets and promoting their development. Since its creation, SEBI has sought to improve the structure and functioning of stock exchanges and to ensure disclosure and investor protection. SEBI has issued comprehensive guidelines called Securities and Exchange Board of India (Disclosure and Investor Protection) Guidelines, 2000. These Guidelines deal with various aspects like listing requirement, promoters' contribution, offer document, advertisement, allotment of shares, etc. They are applicable to all public issues by listed and unlisted companies, all offers for sale and rights issues by listed companies whose equity share capital is listed, except in case of rights issues where the aggregate value of securities offered does not exceed Rs. 50 lacs. These guidelines have been revised vide Circular No. 11, dated August 14, 2003.

The National Stock Exchange

NSE was established in 1994 as a competitor to the Bombay Stock Exchange (BSE). NSE was backed by major financial institutions, led by the Industrial Development Bank of India. The exchange introduced nationwide screen-based trading with a dish-to-satellite data transmission system that provides instant trading access to brokers anywhere in India. NSE forced BSE and other exchanges to adapt by upgrading to computerized systems and by reforming trading rules and procedures.

Clearance, Settlement and the National Securities Depository

In mid-1996 NSE began guaranteeing execution of trades through a new clearing corporation. This removed a major risk that had always been present in the past and forced BSE to respond with improved clearance procedures. In late 1996, the National Securities Depository Limited was inaugurated. NSDL is gradually providing a means by which securities trading will take place using electronic means. An earlier proposal for a depository that would hold physical shares had been under development for several years, but the Indian securities industry decided to forgo the costs of storing physical shares and created a depository for "dematerialized" shares. Trading takes place in both physical and dematerialized shares, but SEBI now requires institutions to trade only in the latter form. (Shah 1998)

Some of other specific measures taken for protection of investors include:

- "Investor's guidance services" of SEBI to guide and educate the investors about grievances and remedies available to them.
- Disciplinary Action committees have been set-up in each stock exchange to take up complaints against companies, brokers, etc.
- SEBI has revised the required disclosure guidelines to give more details of accounts and other related mattes.
- SEBI has issued specific guidelines to deal with bad deliveries.
- Each stock exchange is under a legal obligation to create an investor protection fund to compensate the investors for losses suffered by them due to default on part of stock exchanges.
- Investors have been permitted to form associations and register them under SEBI. These associations are expected to promote interest of investors by making them aware about various issues.

SECTION 2

This section deals with the analysis of the data collected regarding awareness of investors about SEBI guidelines regarding brokers, sources of information of investor protection guidelines and problems faced by investors.

Period of making Investment

The respondents were asked about the period of making investment, i.e. since how long they have been making investments. As shown in Table 1, 40.67 percent respondents were making investments for less than five years. 40 percent were making investments for a period between five to ten years. 13.33 percent for ten to fifteen and 6 percent for fifteen to twenty years. Hence, majority of respondents were making investments for the last ten years.

TABLE I

Period of making Investments

Period (years)	*Number of Respondents*	*Percentage*
0-5	61	40.67
5-10	60	40.00
10-15	20	13.33
15-20	9	6.00
Total	150	100.00

Number of Institutions the Respondents made Investments

The respondents were asked to give the number of institutions they have made investments in. Table 2 shows that 36 percent respondents invested in less than ten institutions, 25.33 percent invested in ten to twenty institutions and 23.33 percent invested in twenty to thirty institutions. The number of investors who invested in more than thirty institutions was only sixteen percent. The majority of investors invested in less than twenty institutions.

Services of Brokers

The respondents were asked to indicate whether they availed the services of brokers while making investments in primary and secondary markets. As revealed by Table 3,

TABLE 2

Number of Institutions the Respondents made Investments

Institutions	*Number of Respondents*	*Percentage*
0-10	54	36.00
10-20	38	25.33
20-30	35	23.33
30-40	7	4.67
40-50	9	6.00
Above 50	7	4.67
Total	150	100.00

large majority of respondents, i.e. 76 percent availed the services of brokers while making investments in secondary market, 55.33 percent of investors availed services of brokers while making investment in the primary market. Although majority of investors availed services of brokers in secondary as well as in primary market yet there was a good number of investors who did not get the services of brokers.

TABLE 3

Services of Brokers

Market	*Number of Respondents*	*Percentage*
Primary Market	83	55.33
Secondary Market	114	76.00

Knowledge about Registration of Brokers

The registration of brokers has been made compulsory by SEBI. The respondents were asked about the awareness of registration of brokers. Table 4 indicates that majority of investors, i.e. 78.67 percent had knowledge about the fact that registration of brokers has been made compulsory. Only 21.33 percent respondents were not aware about the mandatory registration of brokers.

TABLE 4

Knowledge about Registration of Brokers

Knowledge	*Number of Respondents*	*Percentage*
Yes	118	78.67
No	32	21.33
Total	150	100.00

Registration of Brokers

The respondents were asked to point out whether the broker with whom they were dealing was registered or not. Table 5 shows that the majority of the respondents availed the services of registered brokers. Only 14.41 percent availed the services of unregistered brokers.

TABLE 5

Registration of Brokers

Registration	*Number of Respondents*	*Percentage*
Yes	101	85.59
No	17	14.41
Total	118	100.00

Awareness of SEBI Guidelines

Table 6 shows that 52.67 respondents were aware about

TABLE 6

Awareness of SEBI Guidelines

Awareness	*Number of Respondents*	*Percentage*
Yes	79	52.67
No	71	47.33
Total	150	100.00

the SEBI guidelines for brokers and 47.33 were not aware. Hence awareness about guidelines issued by SEBI for brokers was average.

Compliance of SEBI Guidelines

The respondents who were aware about SEBI guidelines for brokers were asked to give their response about the compliance of SEBI guidelines by brokers. 52.67 percent of investors were aware about these guidelines. 54.47 percent of the above respondents were of the view that the brokers generally follow the SEBI guidelines. 29.11 percent investors felt that brokers rarely follow the guidelines. 10.12 percent of the investors were of the opinion that brokers always follows the guidelines. Only 6.30 percent felt that brokers never follow the guidelines.

TABLE 7

Compliance of SEBI Guidelines

Compliance	*Number of Respondents*	*Percentage*
Always	8	10.13
Often	43	54.47
Rarely	23	29.11
Never	5	6.30
Total	79	100.00

Effect of Non-compliance on Investment Decisions

The respondents were asked about the effect of non-compliance of guidelines on their investment decisions. As indicated by Table 8 the majority of respondents, i.e. 68 percent were of the view that there was no effect on investment decisions. 32 percent investors felt that investment decisions were affected by non-compliance of SEBI guidelines.

Sources of Information for Investors' Protection Guidelines

The investors were asked about the sources from which they got the information regarding investor protection guidelines. The investors used different sources of

TABLE 8

Effect of Non-compliance on Investment Decisions

Effect	*Number of Respondents*	*Percentage*
Yes	48	32.00
No	102	68.00
Total	150	100.00

information for investor protection guidelines. The majority of investors, i.e. 76 percent used newspaper for getting this information. 61.33 percent of the respondents got the information from journals/magazines, T.V. News/reports were used by 40.67 percent respondents. The least used source of information was friends/relatives, i.e. 23.33 percent. Hence newspapers and journals/magainzes were the most important sources of information for investor protection guidelines.

TABLE 9

Sources of Information for Investors' Protection Guidelines

Sources	*Number of Respondents*	*Percentage*
Newspapers	114	76.00
Journals/Magazines	92	61.33
T.V. News/Reports	61	40.67
Agents/Brokers	56	37.33
Friends/Relatives	35	23.33

Awareness of about 'Investor Protection Bodies

The respondents were asked to name the bodies available for protecting the interests of investors. The investors named different bodies for investor protection. As revealed by Table 10 the majority of respondents, i.e. 72 percent named SEBI as investor protection body. 24 percent respondents named Reserve Bank of India and 14.67 percent named Company Law Board as investor protection body. Only 6 percent investors named three bodies investor association, registrar of companies and stock exchanges as investor protection bodies. Hence, from the investors' view point SEBI is the most important body for the protection of investors.

TABLE 10

Awareness of about Investor Protection Bodies

Body	*Number of Respondents*	*Percentage*
SEBI	108	72
RBI	36	24.
CLB	22	14.67
Consumer Courts	13	8.67
Investor Association	4	2.67
ROC	3	2.00
Stock Exchange	2	1.33

Respondents' Satisfaction about Guidelines

The SEBI has issued guidelines covering different areas for the efficient functioning of capital market. The investors were given different areas for which SEBI issued guidelines and were asked to respond on the five point Likert Scale about their satisfaction level. As indicated by Table 11 regarding the disclosure of information in case of public issues and right issues, 32 percent were satisfied, 17.33 percent were highly satisfied, 23.33 percent were neutral, 22.67 percent were dissatisfied and 4.67 percent respondents were highly dissatisfied with the guidelines.

The weighted average score of 0.346 indicates that the investors' level of satisfaction was quite high.

As far as norms for issue of stock invest were concerned, 17.33 percent investors were highly satisfied, 27.33 percent were satisfied, 25.33 percent were neutral, 27.33 percent were dissatisfied, and only 2.67 percent investors were highly dissatisfied. The weighted average score of 0.293 showed that the investors were satisfied only to some extent with these norms.

'TABLE 11

Respondents' Satisfaction about Guidelines

Guidelines	*HS*	*S*	*NSND*	*DS*	*HDS*	*WAS*
(i) Disclosure of information in case of public issues and right issues	26	48	35	34	7	0.346
	(17.33)	(32.00)	(23.33)	(22.67)	(4.67)	
(ii) Norms for issue of stock invest	26	41	38	41	4	0.293
	(17.33)	(27.33)	(25.33)	(27.33)	(2.67)	
(iii) Rules for bonus shares	12	66	36	33	3	0.34
	(8.00	(44.00)	(24.00)	(22.00)	(2.00)	
(iv) Rules for refund of application money	6	44	29	46	25	-0.266
	(4.0)	(29.33)	(19.33)	(30.67)	(16.67)	
(v) Rules for share transfers	1	51	29	51	18	-0.226
	(0.67)	(34.00)	(19.33)	(34.00)	(12.00)	
(vi) Redressal of Grievances	3	24	33	60	30	-0.6
	(2.00)	(16.00)	(22.00)	(40.00)	(20.00)	
(vii) Norms for insider trading	1	17	48	50	34	-0.66
	(0.67)	(11.00)	(32.00)	(33.33)	(22.67)	
(viii) Guidelines for the protection of interest of debenture holders	8	12	38	61	31	-0.633
	(5.33)	(8.00)	(25.33)	(40.67)	(20.67)	

8 percent respondents were highly satisfied with rules for bonus shares, 44 percent were satisfied, 24 percent were neutral, 22 percent were dissatisfied and only 2 percent were highly dissatisfied. The weighted average score of 0.34 revealed that the investors were more satisfied with the rules for bonus shares as compared to norms for issue of stock invest.

30.67 percent respondent were dissatisfied with rules for refund for application money, 29.33 percent were satisfied, 19.33 percent were neutral, 16.67 percent were highly dissatisfied and only 4 percent respondents were highly satisfied. The weighted average score of –0.266 revealed that the majority of investors were dissatisfied with the rules for refund of application money.

As far as rules for transfer of shares were concerned, 34 percent investors were satisfied, 19.33 percent were neutral, 34 percent were dissatisfied, 12 percent were highly dissatisfied and only 0.67 percent were highly satisfied. The weighted average score of –0.226 showed that the investors were dissatisfied with the rules for transfer of shares.

40 percent investors were dissatisfied with the guidelines for redressal of grievances, 20 percent were highly dissatisfied, 22 percent were neutral, 16 percent were satisfied and 2 percent were highly satisfied. The weighted average score of –0.6 revealed that the majority of investors were dissatisfied.

As far as norms for insider trading were concerned, 33.33 percent respondents were dissatisfied, 22.67 percent were highly dissatisfied, 32 percent were neutral, 11.33 percent were satisfied, and only 0.67 percent were highly satisfied. The weighted average score of –0.66 showed that the majority of investors were dissatisfied with the norms for insider trading.

Regarding the guidelines for interest payment to debenture holders in case of default in making allotment of issue in time by the company, 40.67 percent respondents were dissatisfied, 20.67 were highly dissatisfied, 25.33 percent were neutral, 8 percent were satisfied and 5.33 percent were highly satisfied. The weighted average of –0.633 indicated that the investors were not satisfied with these guidelines.

Hence we conclude that the investors' level of satisfaction was near to average for guidelines for disclosure of information for public issue and right issue, norms for issue of stock invest, and rules for bonus shares. However, the respondents were dissatisfied with the norms for insider trading, redressal of grievances, rules for share transfer, rules for refund of application money and rules for interest payment to debenture holders.

Problems Faced by Investors

The investors face different types of problems while dealing in securities. They were given different problems and asked to rank them in accordance with their severity. As revealed by Table 12 rank 1 was given to problem of long time taken to register share transfer. Hence this was the major problem faced by respondents. The problem of delay in allotment of shares got the weighted average score of 810 and was ranked second. Third rank was given to the problem of refund of application money. The least important problem was delay in receiving dividend/interest.

TABLE 12

Problems Faced by Investors

Problem	*WAS*	*Rank*
Long time taken is allotment of shares	810	2
Refund of application money	784	3
Long time taken to register share transfer	839	1
Insider Trading	395	7
Insufficient information regarding performance of the company	611	4
Buying and selling of shares	497	6
Delay in receiving Share/Debenture certificate	518	5
Delay in receiving divided/interest	274	8

Note: Weighted Average Score (WAS) was calculated by assigning weights of 8 for rank 1, 7 for rank 2 and 1 for rank 8.

Registration of Complaints

The respondents were asked to tell whether they have written any complaint against the companies or other institutions to SEBI. Table 13 indicates that the majority of respondents, i.e. 63.33 percent have not written any complaint to SEBI. Only 36.67 percent respondents registered complaints against the companies to SEBI. The majority of investor do not register complaints because it takes very long time to resolve the problem. Some investors pointed out that they have no trust in SEBI so far as the redressal of complaints is concerned.

TABLE 13

Registration of Complaints

Registration	*Number of Respondents*	*Percentage*
Yes	55	36.67
No	95	63.33
Total	150	100.00

Time for Getting First Reply from SEBI

The time taken for getting first reply from SEBI against the complaint made by investors has been shown in Table 14, 41.82 percent investors got the reply between two to four weeks, 27.27 percent got reply within two weeks and four to six weeks time was taken by SEBI to send reply for 7.27 percent respondents. Hence the majority of respondents got the reply within four weeks of their complaints.

TABLE 14

Time for Getting First Reply from SEBI

Time (weeks)	*Number of Respondents*	*Percentage*
0-2	15	27.27
2-4	23	41.82
4-6	4	7.27
6-8	7	12.73
Above 8	6	10.91
Total	55	100.00

SEBI's Response to Complaints

The investors were asked about the response of SEBI regarding the complaints registered by them. They were given four responses to tick whichever applicable. As revealed by Table 15 on the complaints of 60 percent respondents, SEBI wrote to the concerned company. The complaints of 25.45 percent investors were pending. The complaints of 10.91 percent respondents were resolved by the efforts of SEBI. No action was taken by SEBI on the complaints of 3.64 percent respondents. We can conclude that on an average, nearly 11 percent complaints of investors are settled by the SEBI. In case of most of the complaints the SEBI only writes to the concerned company which does not seems to bother much about the SEBI guidelines.

TABLE 15

SEBI's Response to Complaints

Response	*Number of Respondents*	*Percentage*
No action taken	2	3.64
Issue still pending	14	25.45
SEBI has written to the concerned company	33	60.00
Problem has been resolved by SEBI	6	10.91
Total	55	100.00

Time taken by SEBI to Resolve the Problem

42 investors gave their response about the time taken by SEBI to solve their problems. As indicated by Table 16 the problem of 54.76 percent respondents were resolved within two months by the SEBI. The problem of 26.19 percent were resolved by SEBI by taking time between two to four months. SEBI took four to six months time for resolving problems of 11.90 percent investors. SEBI took more than six months time in resolving problems of 7.15 percent investors.

Adequacy of Administration of SEBI

The respondents were asked to give response regarding the adequacy of administration of SEBI. As indicated by

TABLE 16

Time taken by SEBI to Resolve the Problem

Time (months)	*Number of Respondents*	*Percentage*
0-2	23	54.76
2-4	11	26.19
4-6	5	11.90
Above 6	3	7.15

Table 17, 50.67 percent investors pointed out that the administration of SEBI was not adequate to safeguard the interest of the large number of investors. But 49.33 percent were of the view that the administration of SEBI was adequate. For improvement in the administration of SEBI it was suggested by investors that more offices should be opened and powers should be decentralised.

TABLE 17

Adequacy of Administration of SEBI

Adequacy	*Number of Respondents*	*Percentage*
Yes	74	49.33
No	76	50.67
Total	150	100.00

CONCLUSION

The percent study was conducted with the objective to examine the awareness and protection of investors in light to the various measures taken by government and SEBI. Following conclusions were drawn:

- Most of the investors are making investments in securities for the last ten years and they believed in diversification of their investments.

- Majority of investors take services of brokers while making their investments both in the primary as well as secondary market. But investors are more dependent on brokers in secondary market.
- Majority of the investors knew about compulsory registration of brokers and they prefer to deal with such brokers. Very thin majority believes that brokers often follow the guidelines laid by SEBI but their failure to comply with such guidelines do not affect investment decision of majority investors.
- Newspapers and journals/magazines are most important sources for investors to become aware of measures taken for their protection.
- Most of investors look towards SEBI as their savior.
- The satisfaction level of investors was average about the guidelines for disclosure of information in café of public issues and right issues, norms for issue of stock invest and rules for bonus shares. They were highly dissatisfied in case of redressal of grievances and norms for insider trading.
- Two major problems faced by investors relate to delay in registering share transfer, and allotment of shares.
- Investors generally register their complaints, if any, with SEBI which in most of cases is furthered to the concerned company by it.
- Majority of investors feel that administration of SEBI is not adequate and they demand that more offices of SEBI should be opened in various parts of country and powers be decentralised.

References

Agarwal, Krishna Kumar, *New Issue Market Operations in India*, Kanishka Publishers, Distributors, New Delhi, 1997.

Anuj, "Investors' Protection in India", *Business Analyst*, Vol. 12, No. 1, July-Dec. 1991, pp. 85-91.

Avadhani, V.A., *SEBI Guidelines and Listing of Securities*, Himalaya Publishing House, Mumbai, 1996.

Bhadada, B.M., "Protecting the Indian Corporate Investor through Effective Regulation", as quoted in Lalwani, Sushil, J. (ed.), *Security Market in*

India, Book Treasure, Jodhpur, 1995, pp. 240-46.

Chander, Subash and Singh, Balwinder, "SEBI and Investor Protection" as quoted in Lalwani Sushil, J. (ed.), *Security Market in India*, Book Treasure, Jodhpur, 1995, pp. 257-66.

Chitale, Rajendra P., "Regulatory Framework for Securities Market", *Chartered Secretary*, Vol, XXV, No. 10, October 1995, pp. 942-51.

Fox, James W., Developing the Capital Market in India, USAID's Development Experience, Clearing House, Arlington, 1999.

Gordon, E., Natrajan, K., "Capital Market in India", Himalaya Publishing House, Mumbai, 1999, pp. 130-31.

Goswami, Deep, "SEBI's Newly Acquired Powers to Prosecute Companies Neglecting Investor Protection", *Chartered Secretary*, Vol. XXIV, No. 3, March 1994, p. 205.

Gupta, L.C., *Indian Shareholders—A Survey, Society for Capital Market Research and Development*, Delhi 1991.

Gupta, Sunita, "Mutual Funds *Vs.* Investors' Protection" as quoted in Lalwani, Sushil, J. (ed.), *Security Market in India*, Book Treasure, Jodhpur, 1995, pp. 639-41.

Mayya, M.R., "Investor Protection" , *The Stock Exchange Review*, June 1996, pp. 5-26.

Mishra, B.M., "Fifty Years of the Indian Capital Market : 1947-97", *Reserve Bank of India, Occasional Papers*, Vol. 18, Nos. 2 & 3, June & September 1997, pp. 351-83.

Nair, T.R.C., "Investor Protection Measures and Formalities to be Complied with by Companies in Connection with Public Issues", *Chartered Secretary*, Vol. XXI, No. 4, April 1991, pp. 295-96.

Narta, S.S., *Capital Issues in India*, Kanishka Publishing House, Delhi, 1992.

Shah, Ajay, "Institutional Changes in India's Capital Markets", Nov. 23, 1998.

Shah, Ajay, Thomas, Susan, Policy Issues in India's Capital Market in 2000 A.D.

Srivastava, S.P., "Protecting the Investors", *Chartered Accountant*, Vol. XLII, No. 11, May 1994, pp. 977-79.

Srivastava, S.S., "Investment Opportunities and Investor Protection in India", as quoted in Lalwani, Sushil, J. (ed.), *Security Market in India*, Book Treasure, Jodhpur, 1995, pp. 109-117.

Thakur, K.S., Singh, B.K. and Singh, S.K., "Growth of Indian Stock Market : Problems and Prescriptions", *The Indian Journal of Commerce*, Vol. XLVII, No. 181, December 1994, pp. 111-14.

www.sebi.gov.in

www.rbi.org.in

www.dec.org/usaid_eval

2

Capital Market Reforms

A Case Study of Grievances and Awareness of Retail Investors in Stock Market*

PAWAN KUMAR TANEJA AND P.P. SINGH

INTRODUCTION

Investors are the backbone of the security markets. It is the investor who buys and sells securities without which the security market would not exist. They are the soul of the capital market. An investor is very much needed because he is the major (rather the only) source of providing risk capital. As Portfolio Managers (like Mutual Funds) fill their baskets on the basis of subjective evaluation of scrip and foreign institutional investors are busy pocketing profit by only investing in profitable companies. Hence, none of them is interested in injecting much-needed risk capital. Thus the task is only left to retail investors. But number of investors and volume of investment made by these risk capital providers is very less. After various scams are related to security market

* Paper for Presentation at the National Seminar on Capital Market Reforms in India Organized by Department of Commerce & Business Management, Guru Nanak Dev University, Amritsar, 1st-2nd March 2004.

(like 1992 Scam (Harshad Mehta), JVG Scam etc.) the level of investment volume and number of investors is continuously declining due to following factors:

(1) Whenever any retail investor faces an institutional failure he does not get help from any quarter and has to accept it as a bad luck.
(2) The scams remain under investigation with no concrete steps taken against defunct companies and have to accept it as a part of Investment risk.
(3) Regulators and financial intermediaries only highlight the value addition of new intermediaries, new instruments and new system of trading but nobody discloses inherent risk.

CAPITAL MARKET REFORMS

For the fulfilment of the basic task of securities market to help in process of capital formation in the economy, the investors need to be lured back into the market. This can only be possible by series of systematic measures which would build their confidence in the systems and processes, and protect their interest fully, continues education of investors regarding their rights and new techniques and technology. Realizing its importance the Ministry of Finance had taken various important steps to bring/lure the retail investor back into the market. These steps are popularly known as "Capital Market Reforms".

Some of the noticeable reforms are:

- The Capital Issues (Control) Act, 1947, repealed, office of the Controller of Capital Issues abolished and initial share pricing decontrolled.
- The SEBI (Securities and Exchange Board of India), the capital market regulator, established in 1992. The primary function of SEBI is to regulate the capital markets and protect the interest of the investors. The other important functions of SEBI are:
  - o Regulating the business in stock exchanges and

any other securities markets.
  - o Registering and regulating the working of collective investment schemes, including mutual funds.
  - o Prohibiting fraudulent and unfair trade practices relating to securities markets.
  - o Promoting investor's education and training of intermediaries of securities markets.
  - o Prohibiting insider trading in securities, with the imposition of monetary penalties, on erring market intermediaries.
  - o Regulating substantial acquisition of shares and takeover of companies.
  - o Calling for information from, carrying out inspection, conducting inquiries and audits of the stock exchanges and intermediaries and self-regulatory organizations in the securities market.
- Foreign institutional investors (FIIs) are allowed to invest in Indian capital markets after registration with the SEBI.
- Indian companies permitted to access international capital markets through euro issues.
- The National Stock Exchange (NSE), with nationwide stock trading and electronic display, clearing and settlement facilities, established. Several regional stock exchanges change over from floor-based trading to screen-based trading.
- SEBI regulations governing substantial acquisition of shares and takeovers, including conditions under which disclosures and mandatory public offers are to be made to shareholders.
- Private mutual funds permitted.
- The Depositories Act provides a legal framework for the establishment of depositories to record ownership deals in book entry form. Dematerialization of stocks encourages paperless trading.
- Companies are required to disclose all material facts and specific risk factors associated with their

projects while making public issues.

- To reduce the cost of issue, underwriting by the issuer made optional, subject to conditions.
- The practice of making preferential allotment of shares at prices unrelated to the prevailing market prices stopped and fresh guidelines issued by SEBI.
- SEBI reconstitutes governing boards of the stock exchanges, introduces capital adequacy norms for brokers, and makes rules for making client/broker relationship more transparent, including separation of client and broker accounts.
- Single time permission to stockbrokers extended to corporatise their business, without attracting capital gains tax.
- Buy back of shares allowed.
- The SEBI starts insisting on greater corporate disclosures. Steps being taken to improve corporate governance based on the report of a committee.
- SEBI issues detailed employee stock option scheme and employee stock purchase scheme for listed companies.
- Standard denomination for equity shares of Rs. 10 and Rs. 100 abolished. Companies given the freedom to issue dematerialized shares in any denomination.
- Derivatives trading starts with index options and futures.
- Depository system has been established to eliminate the weaknesses of traditional physical or paper form of shares system.
- A system of rolling settlements introduced.
- SEBI empowered to register and regulate venture capital funds.
- The SEBI (Credit Rating Agencies) Regulations, 1999 issued for regulating new credit rating agencies as well as introducing a code of conduct for all credit rating agencies operating in India.
- Badla system has been abolished.

Keeping this in view, SEBI has issued a new set of

comprehensive guidelines governing issue of shares and other financial instruments, and has laid down detailed norms for stock-brokers and sub-brokers, merchant bankers, portfolio managers and mutual funds. SEBI defined the rights and responsibilities of the shareholders and also takes certain steps towards investor's education and set-up framework for removal of their grievances.

SEBI EFFORTS TOWARDS INVESTOR'S EDUCATION

1. It has launched intensive investor education exercises.
2. Helps investor in Redressal of complaints.
3. Disseminates information through its website.
4. Published number of booklets on policy developments for educating the investors.
5. It distributed booklets titled "A Quick Reference Guide for Investors".
6. Issued a series of advertisements/public issues in national as well as regional newspapers to educate and caution the investor about the risks associated with the collective investment schemes.
7. SEBI registered investor association's organized seminars for educating investors on various aspects relating to market.

REFORMS REGARDING GRIEVANCE REDRESSAL

In the reform process it is clearly defined the various authorities that will be accountable for and will be redressing various kinds of the grievances:

Nature of Grievance	*Can be taken up with*
In case of any Public Issue, non-receipt of:	
• Refund order	• SEBI
• Interest on delayed refund	• Deptt. of Company Affairs
• Allotment advice	• Deptt. of Company Affairs
• Share certificates	• Stock Exchange
• Duplicates for all of the above	• Registrars to the issue
• Re-validations	• Registrars to the issue

In case of a listed security, non-receipt of the certificates after: • Transfer • Transmission • Conversion • Endorsement • Consolidation • Splitting • Duplicates of securities	 • SEBI • SEBI • SEBI • Deptt. of Company Affairs • Stock Exchange • Stock Exchange • Stock Exchange
Regarding listed Debentures, non-receipt of • Interest due • Redemption proceeds • Interest on delayed payment	 • SEBI • Deptt. of Company Affairs • The Debenture Trustees/Stock Exchange
• Regarding bad delivery of shares • Regarding shares or debentures in Unlisted companies • Deposits in collective investment schemes like plantations etc. • Units of Mutual Funds • Fixed Deposits in Banks and Finance Companies • Fixed Deposits in manufacturing companies	• Delivery cell of the stock exchange. • Deptt. of Company Affairs • SEBI • SEBI • Reserve Bank of India • Deptt. of Company Affairs

Investor Information Centers have been set-up in every recognized stock exchange which in addition to the complaints to the securities traded/listed with them, will take up all other complaints regarding the trades effected in the exchange and the relevant member of the exchange.

Some other steps for investor's grievances redressal are:

- Investor Grievances Cell
- Investor Protection Fund
- Investor Service Fund
- Complaints with Consumers' Disputes Redressal Forums
- Suits in the Court of Law.

NEED OF THE STUDY

Indian capital market has witnessed a massive growth in last decade with the introduction of non-interventionist reconstruction measures. The Government of India has taken various measures for investor education to streamline the escalating capital market to cope with the changing business equations. However, the dilemmas are:

- Is investor aware about these steps? If yes, what is his perception regarding these?
- What are different kinds of problems faced by the investors since these reforms?
- And from where the investor is redressed in such a case?
- What are their suggestions for making these steps communicated to them, as it should be?

In this paper we are trying to explore out the answers of all the above questions.

DATA AND METHODOLOGY

As this study is exploratory in nature, data for this study is basically primary in nature. For the purpose of the study, a sample of 100 retail investors who are visiting Ludhiana Stock Exchange is taken. A well-structured questionnaire is supplied to investors and they are personally interviewed to share their experiences in stock market dealing, educational programs attended by them and to know their grievances. For the purpose of analysis of data appropriate statistical techniques are used.

RESULTS AND DISCUSSIONS

Profile of Respondents

Age Group

From following table, it is very much clear that most of the investors, i.e. 45% are young. This reaffirm the fact that

Age (in yrs)	*Respondents*
18-40	45%
40-60	30%
60 & above	25%

most of young investors are keen to fill their pockets quickly and they are always more learnt than the higher age group investors who are mainly interested in steady secured income through dividends and capital gains.

Investment Level

Investment/month	*Respondents*
Up to Rs. 1 Lakh	30%
Rs. 1-3 Lakh	37%
Above Rs.3 Lakh	33%

From the above table it is clear that our sample choice is a balance one as the respondents in all the categories of levei of investment are almost same.

Experience of the Respondent in the Stock Market

Experience	*Respondents*
Less than 1 year	7.5%
1-2 years	12.5%
2-3 years	10%
Above 3 years	70%

The above table clearly shows that most of the respondents have been in the market for fairly long period of time and this shows their keen interest in the market. 70% of the respondents have been in the market for more than three years, 12.5% of the respondents have been in the market for 1-2 years. 10% of the respondents have been in the market for two to three years followed by 7.5% being there for less than a year.

Investment Preferences

Instruments	*Respondents*
Equity	77%
Debentures	13%
Bonds	10%

From above we see that equity shares are the most favoured instruments amongst the investors. The possible reason for this might be that investors may believe in the theory "higher the risk higher will be the expected return." (Equity shares are the most risky securities). In addition, the earlier table shows that most of the respondents are in the age group of less than 40 yrs who are normally interested in higher risk securities.

Investor Grievances

Problems in Trading/Exchange

Problem	*Respondents*
Faced	60%
Not Faced	40%

From the above data it is clear that more number of the respondents are facing problems in the trading and transactions. This may be due to either the unawareness or little knowledge concerning the online trading system or capital sector reforms.

Nature of Problems being Faced

Problem	*Respondents*
Non-transfer of shares	60%
Delayed delivery of shares	55%
Non-receipt of dividend	50%
Non-receipt of redemption proceeds	40%
Any other	35%

From the above multiple-choice analysis we conclude that, out of the 60% respondents who faced problems (refer to previous table), the frequent problems that the respondents faced were of non-transfer of shares and late delivery of shares. The problem of non-receipt of redemption proceeds and dividend seems to increase because of many sick companies getting them listed. The other problems faced by the investors are as follows:

- Non-receipt of Annual Report.
- Non-receipt of interest ands bonds.
- No intimation of annual general meeting by companies.
- Company changing name and address without intimation.
- Share certificates neither accepted nor rejected.

Action Pursued

Following course of action is normally taken by investor to redress his problem:

(a) Presenting document again and again.
(b) Approached Stock Exchange for lodging the complaint.
(c) Written to the company, stock brokers and SEBI to resolve it.
(d) Repeated reminders.
(e) Went to court.

The above action taken by the respondents clearly indicate that they have either reported to stock exchange or to the registrar of the company. They even sent reminders to companies to take action. Only a few have went to the court or to SEBI.

Investors' Awareness

Investors' Awareness and Education Program

Level of Awareness of Investors

Response	*Respondents*
Yes	95%
No	5%

Almost all the respondents are aware of the programs, which are run by various stock exchanges, which might be due to the fact that investors want to protect themselves from the fraudulent activities. Only 5% of the respondents are not aware of the investor education programs being run by various exchanges.

Programs Awareness

Programs	*Respondents*
Seminars	70%
Project/Research Activities	4%
Booklets/Brochures	40%
Advertisements	50%

The programs which the investors are maximum aware is the seminars as 70% investors are aware of the seminars. Investors might have preferred seminars, as seminars are more interactive. They can counter-question plus they can solve their queries on the spot. Also 50% (of 95% respondents who are aware of the various programs) are aware about the advertisements and 40% are aware of the booklets/brouchres. Of the projects/research activities they are the least aware, i.e., only 4% are aware which may be due to the fact that investors do not invest in a professional manner.

Investor Awareness and Investors' Right Protection Cells/Funds

The cell which the investors are maximum aware of is

Organizations	*Respondents*
Investor Service Cell	70%
Investor Grievance Redressal System	68%
Investor Protection Fund	55%
Trade Guarantee Fund	32%
Settlement Guarantee Fund	37%

the investor service cell which may be due to the fact that it is the run under the exchange's administration. 70% of the investors are aware of the Investor Service Cell, followed by 68% knowing about Grievance Redressal System, 55% knowing about Investor Protection Fund, 37% knowing about Settlement Guarantee Fund and 13% being aware of the Trade Guarantee Fund.

Precautions	*Respondents*
Not dealing with unregistered intermediary	85%
Giving clear instructions to intermediaries	72%
Keeping a record of all the instructions received	63%
Not dealing in speculative trading	60%
Maximum brokerage that can be charged by the broker	67%
Period for filing complaint	37%
Format for filing complaint	35%

Investors' Awareness regarding Precautions for Selection of Market Intermediaries

The above table shows that investors are aware of most of the precautions that they should take before selecting broker/sub-broker, except a few. As 85% of them are aware of the fact that they should deal only with registered broker, 72% know the fact that they have to give clear instructions to brokers and 63% are aware of the fact that they have to keep a complete record of instructions. 67% of the respondents are only aware of the maximum brokerage that can be charged by investors while only 37% know about the period of filing complaint and 35% know of the format of filing complaint.

Investors' Awareness regarding their Rights and Responsibilities

73% investors are aware of their rights and responsibilities.

Response	*Respondents*
Yes	67%
No	33%

Investors' Awareness regarding Moves and Measures Undertaken by Investor Protection Organizations

The above table shows that average investors are only aware of the various moves and measures undertaken by various investor organizations. Only 67% are aware of the moves and measures and 33% are not aware.

Avenues	*Respondents*
Stock Exchange	80%
Company Law Board	50%
ROC	35%
SEBI	75%
RBI	27%

Investors' Awareness to Avenues for Lodging Complaints

The table clearly shows that the investors are maximum aware about the existence of stock exchange, SEBI and company law board. 80% of the respondents are aware of the existence of Stock Exchange as an avenue available for lodging complaint, whereas 50% know about Company Law Board, 35% being aware of ROC, 75% being aware of SEBI and 27% being aware of RBI.

Investors' Perception

Perception and Investors' Educational Program

Rating the Effectiveness

The above table clearly shows that the investors have rated the above programs launched by various exchanges as

Rating	*Respondents*
Good	82%
Bad	0%
Neutral	18%

good, which means that the exchanges have really taken an effort to educate the investors. 82% have rated them as good and 18% have given no response. It is interesting to know that no one has rated them as bad.

Benefits Gained from the Various Education Programs

Awareness Regarding	*Respondents*
Investor Rights	80%
Investor Protection Funds	28%
Various Redressal Organizations	45%
Procedure to Resolve Complaints	25%

The major benefit derived out by the 95% of total respondents who are aware of the various investor education programs and across these programs awareness of investor rights, which clearly shows that programs mainly focused on investor rights. As 80% of the respondents gained knowledge about their rights, 45% gained about various Redressal organizations, 28% came to know about various Investor Protection Funds and 25% became aware of the procedure how to solve complaints. This trend may be due to as earlier stated that most of the respondents are at come across the mainly seminars, advertisement and brochures, which generally provide information of theoretical nature not the procedural knowledge.

Perception regarding Programs Conducted by LSE last year

Most of the respondents have rated the program as good. It means they are positive attitude towards these programs. These may be beneficial to them.

Investors' Perception and Grievance Redressal

Rating	Respondents
Excellent	8%
Good	70%
Fair	18%
Poor	4%

Perception regarding Working of Investors' Protection Organizations

So we can conclude that:

(a) Investor service cell—the investors are satisfied by it's working.
(b) Investor grievance Redressal system—the investors are satisfied by it's working.
(c) Investor protection fund—the investors are dissatisfied.
(d) Trade guarantee fund—the investors are dissatisfied by its working.
(e) Settlement guarantees fund—the investors have an indifferent attitude towards this fund.

	Highly satisfied	Satis- fied	Indiff- erent	Dissatis- fied	Highly Dissatis- fied
Investor Service Cell	12%	70%	9%	6%	3%
Investor Grievance Redressal System	5%	60%	18%	12%	5%
Investor Protection Fund	2%	28%	11%	46%	14%
Trade Guarantee Fund	0%	13%	15%	51%	21%
Settlement Guarantee Fund	1%	21%	57%	18%	3%

Perception regarding Working of Redressal Mechanism of NSE, BSE and LSE

The investors with working of all the three organizations but they are most satisfied by BSE, then NSE and lastly they are also satisfied with the working of LSE.

Investor Perception and Future Course of Action

	Highly Satisfied	*Satisfied*	*Indifferent*	*Dissatisfied*	*Highly Dissatisfied*
BSE	15%	70%	5%	8%	2%
NSE	10%	54%	12%	16%	8%
LSE	11%	50%	19%	11%	9%

Perception for Transference of Investors' Educational Program in Future

It is clearly seen from the above table no respondents has said no to these programs. They all have encouraged these programs.

Response	*Respondents*
Yes	100%
No	0%

Attitude towards Attending these Programs if Organized

It can be clearly seen that majority of investors would attend these programs if organized. 80% of the respondents are ready to attend these programs whereas 20% are not interested to attend these programs.

Response	*Respondents*
Yes	80%
No	20%

Mode Preferred by Investors for Education Programs

The mode, which the investors preferred the most, is the newspaper, seminars or the stock exchange.

Mode	*Respondents*
Television	55%
Newspapers	70%
At the Stock Exchange	68%
Magazines	38%
Seminars	68%

SUGGESTION BY RESPONDENTS

- More awareness campaigns should be launched in smaller towns.
- Strict monitoring of broker actions.
- Heavy monetary penalties to the defaulting parties.
- Proper books should be available at the exchanges.
- Seminars from grass root levels should be started.
- More seminars on derivatives, futures and options should be conducted.
- More interaction with local investor associations of the stock exchanges to improve the system.
- Protection from sick companies.
- The seminars should be conducted by experts.

CONCLUSION

From the above discussions and results we may conclude that the reform process initiated by government is giving fertile results. As this is very clear looking at the awareness level of the retail investors. But the word of caution is that 60% of them are still facing problems. Now the government should take measures further to strengthening the investor grievances cells and simplify the procedural aspect of grievances redressal. Also the capital market reforms have to be translated to the masses in the appropriate manner by considering the media that is more suitable. Not to forget the measures that needs to be taken by the government for making the rest of 20% who wants continuation of the educational programs but not want to attend these programs, which may be due to the uncatchy presentation or undersupplied contents as per them or poor communication of these programs.

References

Bhole, L.M., (1999), *Financial Institutions and Market: Structure, Growth and Innovation,* Tata McGraw Hill, New Delhi.

Gupta, Ramesh, (1999), "Retail Investors," *The Chartered Accountant*, February 1999, pp. 12-18.

Kumar, Sunil, (1998), "Primary Market—Will it Ever Revive," *Dalal Street*, Vol. XII, No. 12, pp. 56-58.

Mehta, Arpana, (2001), "Indian Stock Market Towards Safer Havens," *Chartered Financial Analyst*, June 2001, pp. 49-52.

National Securities Depository Limited, *An Investor's Guide to Depositories.*

National Stock Exchange, *Indian Securities Market: A Review*, Volume IV, 2001.

Pathak, Bharati V., (2003), *Indian Financial System*, Pearson Education (Singapore) Pvt. Ltd., Delhi.

Priyadarshi, Atul, (2000), "Rolling Settlement: Roll over to Efficiency," *Chartered Financial Analyst*, March 2000, pp. 56-58.

Rao, Rashmi, (2002), "The Bite of Reforms," *Capital Market*, January 21-February 3, 2002, pp. 4-8.

Shah, Ajay and Susan Thomas, (1999), "Developing the Indian Capital Market," in Hunson, James A. and Sanjay Kathuria (eds.), *India: A Financail Sector for the Twenty-first Century*, Oxford University Press, Delhi.

Shah, Ajay, (1997), "Security Market Towards Greater Efficiency," in K.S. Parikh (ed.), *India Development Report*, 1997, Delhi, Oxford University Press.

The Economic Times, *The Investors Year Book, 2002.*

www.bseindia.com

www.hinduonnet.com

www.idusinvest.com

www.nseindia.com

www.sebi.gov.in

www.sudhiarlaw.com

Determinants of Futures Pricing

An Econometrical Analysis

SANJEEV SHARMA AND KAPIL GUPTA

INTRODUCTION

Derivatives or Derivative securities are contracts, which are written between two parties and whose value is derived from the value of underlying widely held and easily marketable assets. The underlying assets may be agriculture and other physical (tangible) commodities or currencies or short-term and long-term financial instruments or intangible things like Commodity Price Index (Inflation Index), Equity Price Index or Bond Price Index. Forwards, Futures, Options, Swaps are most commonly used derivatives.

There is no undue restriction on what can constitute an underlying asset except that it has to be objectively observable thus leaving significant scope for automatic inclusion of any new derivative that may be created in future. However, some of the normal transactions have been excluded from being classified as derivative even though futurity and risk may be involved. These include the transactions entered in regular way according to common conventions and trade practices, insurance contracts, bank guarantees, and derivatives that impede a sale contract.

TYPES OF DERIVATIVES

1. Forward Contracts

It is a one to one bi-party contract, to be performed in future, at the terms decided today.

2. Futures

It is an agreement to buy or sell a specified quantity of financial Instruments/commodity for future delivery at an agreed price.

3. Equity Index Futures

Equity Index Futures are a type of financial instruments which are bought or sold with specific motives, e.g., speculation, hedging and arbitraging.

4. Options

Options are the contract between Option Writers (sellers) and the buyer, which obligate the former to deliver, and entitle the latter without obligation to buy stated quantities of assets which stated at some future dates at today's contracted prices (Spot Price) and matures at the strike price on the expiration date. Options can be "Call Option" and "Put Option".

5. Swaps

Swaps are agreements between two parties to exchange assets or set of financial obligations or a series of cash flows for a specified period of time at predetermined intervals.

6. Credit Derivatives

Credit Derivatives are privately negotiated bilateral contracts that allow users to manage their exposure to credit risk. It provides opportunities to enhance yield by purchasing credit systematically.

PRICING OF FUTURES

As discussed earlier, Futures are exchange traded contracts to sell or buy financial instruments or commodities in a designated future month at a price agreed upon by the buyer and seller. A Futures contract is a standardized forward contract.

Futures Pricing Theories

There are many schools of thoughts used to price a Futures contract. These are briefly explained as follows:

1. Expectation Theory

The expectation theory says that only expectations drive the Futures price. In the expectation hypothesis view, Futures prices are forecast of subsequent (expected) cash prices. On an average, the predictions are not biased toward either a consistent positive or negative return.

Thus, the expected profit to either position of a Futures contract equals zero. But supply and demand factors could cause the Futures to be consistently under- or over-priced relative to its true value. This means that the hypothesis that Futures should always be more than the cash price may not hold true if one looks at the expectation theory.

2. The Hedging Pressure Theory

This theory states that Futures price will be less than the expected price when short hedgers outnumber long hedgers. Conversely, Futures price will be greater than expected price when long hedgers outnumber short hedgers. Similarly, when the number of short hedgers equals the number of long hedgers, the Futures price will be equal to the expected price.

3. Cost of Carry Model

This model explains that Futures always have a positive time value owing to the interest cost inbuilt in them for the time remaining to expiration. This model also states that the pricing of Futures contracts and arbitrage between Futures and spot markets are closely related concepts.

Cost of Carry = Interest Charge over the Spot price for the days remaining to expiration

To calculate the Futures price of an underlying asset, one must account for all cash flows, both positive and negative, that will occur during the holding period. The net difference between the positive (income) flows and negative (expense) flows of an underlying is the Basis another commonly used term for cost of carry.

Thus,

Cost of Carry = Income – Expense = Cash Price – Futures Price = Basis

DERIVATIVES IN INDIA

Derivatives are new financial instruments for the Indian Financial Market. Derivatives have been introduced in India in the Year 2000 as per the recommendations of the L.C. Gupta Committee and the trading mechanism has been designed as per the recommendations of J.R. Verma Committee. The trading in Derivatives was started first of all in the Equity Index Futures and later the trading in individual stocks was introduced as per the recommendations of L.C. Gupta Committee. The trading in Equity Index Futures started as on 12th June, 2000 whereas the trading in the Individual Stock Futures started on 9th Nov., 2000 on National Stock Exchange (NSE).

Objectives of the Study

The present study is an econometrical analysis of determinants of Futures pricing in selected companies of National Stock Exchange. The objectives of the study are as follows:

(a) To examine whether existing price of an Equity share has a significant impact on Futures Price.

(b) To examine whether Nifty Index has any bearing on the Nifty Index Futures.

Data Base and Methodology

The study covers 27 companies from National Stock

Exchange in which Futures trading are permissible. It does not cover those companies like Banking companies (except SBI) in which Futures trading were allowed at a later stage.

To study the relationship between the Futures Price and the Existing Price, the period from November, 2000 to December, 2003 is considered because Futures trading in individual companies were allowed by SEBI from 9th November, 2000. However, the relationship between the Nifty Index Futures and Nifty Index is studied for the period starting from 12th June, 2000 to 31st December, 2003 since Index Futures trading was permitted from 12th June, 2000.

The relevant information required for this study have been compiled from the website of NSE (www.nse-india.com). The data has been analysed through applying regression techniques and the significance of impact of various variables are observed on the basis of T-values and F-values.

The following regression equation is used to study the relationship between Futures price of a share and the underlying existing price:

$$FP_t = a + b_1P_t + U_t \qquad (1)$$

where;

FP_t = Futures Price of a share in period 't',
P_t = Existing Price of a share in period 't', and
U_t = Error term.

In order to analyse the relationship between Futures Price and Nifty Index, the following regression equation is used:

$$NF_t = a + b_1N_t + U_t \qquad (2)$$

Where;

NF_t = Nifty Index Futures in period 't',
N_t = Nifty Index in period 't', and
U_t = Error term.

It is to be noted that the first regression equation is used to denote the relationship between the Futures price and its underlying existing price for each company separately. Thus, we have 27 regression equations representing this relationship for 27 companies selected for this study. However, the second regression equation representing the relationship between Nifty Index Futures and Nifty Index is calculated period-wise (Each Period = 3 Months) for the period 12th June, 2000 to 31 December, 2003. There is one regression equation for each quarter. As such, a total of 15 regression equations are obtained showing the relationship between Nifty Index Futures and Nifty Index.

Hypothesis

We take the following two Null Hypothesis:

H_{01} = Futures stocks derive their values from the underlying instrument.

H_{02} = Index Futures derives their values from the underlying Index.

Regression Results

The regression results obtained from equation (1) and (2) are represented in Table 1 and Table 2 respectively.

OBSERVATIONS AND CONCLUSION

From Table 1, we observe that there is a high degree of correlation between Futures price and existing Equity prices. Except for one company (BSES), the relationship between Futures price and Existing Price (b_1) is not statistically significant in remaining 26 companies because calculated values of 't' is less than the tabulated value of 't' (i.e. 1.782 at 5% level of significance). Further, in case of all companies (except VSNL) calculated F-value is less than the tabulated value of F (i.e. 2.6037 at 5% level of significance), which indicates that the two variables (Futures Price and Existing Price) have the same variance. Thus, indicating the acceptance of hypothesis (H_{01}) taken which implies that Futures price of a share is consistent with the price of its underlying

TABLE I

Regression Results → Futures Price : Existing Price

Equation : $FP_t = a + b_1P_t + U_t$

(Period: Nov., 2000-Dec., 2003)

Sr. No.	Future Stock Code on NSE	Correlation Coefficient (r)	Regression Coefficient (b_1)	T-Values (t)	F-Values (F)	R^2
1.	ACC	0.99	0.99	0.018	1.02	0.98
2.	BAJAJ AUTO	0.99	1.01	0.087	1.02	0.98
3.	BHEL	0.99	1.00	0.017	1.01	0.98
4.	BPCL	0.99	1.01	0.014	1.02	0.98
5.	BSES	0.99	1.02	2.496	1.05	0.98
6.	CIPLA	0.99	0.99	-0.146 ←	1.00	0.98
7.	DIGITAL COMP	0.98	0.97	0.145	1.02	0.96
8.	DRREDDY	0.98	1.06	0.056	1.14	0.96
9.	GRASIM	1.00	1.28	0.687	1.63	1.00
10.	HIND LEVER	0.96	0.95	0.247	1.04	0.92
11.	HIND PETRO	0.97	1.04	0.058	1.15	0.94
12.	HINDALCO	0.99	1.24	0.657	1.54	0.98
13.	HDFC	0.97	1.06	0.017	1.17	0.94
14.	ICICI	0.99	1.15	0.012	1.32	0.98
15.	ITC	0.99	1.07	0.144	1.15	0.98
16.	L&T	0.99	1.14	0.205	1.33	0.98
17.	M&M	0.99	1.02	0.087	1.03	0.98
18.	MTNL	0.96	1.06	0.023	1.19	0.92
19.	RANBAXY	0.99	1.01	0.039	1.02	0.98
20.	RELIANCE	0.99	1.03	0.009	1.11	0.98
21.	SATYAM COMP	0.99	1.05	0.009	1.11	0.98
22.	SBIN	0.99	1.02	-0.032 ←	1.05	0.98
23.	TATATEA	0.98	1.10	0.189	1.24	0.96
24.	TATA POWER	1.00	1.33	0.706	1.77	1.00
25.	TELCO	0.99	1.01	0.018	1.02	0.98
26.	TISCO	0.99	1.27	0.588	1.63	0.98
27.	VSNL	0.99	1.02	-0.163 ←	5.897	0.98
	Tabulated Values	—	—	(1.782)	(2.6037)	—

Figures in paranthesis shows their tabulated values.

TABLE 2

Regression Results → Nifty Index Futures : Nifty Index

Equation : $NF_t = a + b_1N_t + U_t$

(Period : 12 June, 2000-Dec., 2003)

Sr. No.	*Quarter Ended*	*Correlation Coefficient (r)*	*Regression Coefficient (b_1)*	*T-Values (t)*		*F-Values (F)*	R^2
1.	June 2000	0.91	0.94	0.07		1.02	0.83
2.	Sept. 2000	0.84	0.96	0.04		1.08	0.71
3.	Dec. 2000	0.98	0.96	0.03		1.07	0.97
4.	Mar. 2001	0.87	1.03	0.01		1.06	0.76
5.	June 2001	0.90	0.99	0.06		1.03	0.81
6.	Sept. 2001	0.96	0.95	0.05		1.10	0.94
7.	Dec. 2001	0.71	1.06	-0.03	←	1.13	0.51
8.	Mar. 2002	1.00	1.03	-0.04	←	1.07	1.00
9.	June 2002	0.99	0.98	0.03		1.05	0.98
10.	Sept. 2002	0.86	0.96	0.05		1.08	0.74
11.	Dec. 2002	0.97	1.02	-0.03	←	1.05	0.95
12.	Mar. 2003	0.67	0.68	0.01		1.49	0.45
13.	June 2003	0.61	1.00	0.01		1.00	0.37
14.	Sept. 2003	1.00	1.10	-0.11	←	1.20	1.00
15.	Dec. 2003	0.98	1.08	-0.09	←	1.17	0.97
	Tabulated Values	—	—	(2.13)		(19.00)	—

Figures in paranthesis shows their tabulated values.

instrument's price.

Similarly, the results of regression equation of Nifty Index Futures on Nifty Index (Table 2) depicts that the hypothesized relationship between these two variables are not statistically significant. Thus, indicating the acceptance of hypothesis (H_{02}) taken which implies that there is no significant difference between the price of Nifty Index Futures and the Nifty Index.

On the basis of above observations the Null Hypothesis (i.e. H_{01} and H_{02}) is accepted indicating that the Futures Prices are dependent upon the price of their underlying instrument. This implies that Equity Futures price is dependent upon the price of individual Equity stock and Nifty Index Futures is dependent upon the Nifty Index.

References

Bhalla, V.K., Investment Management—Security Analysis and Portfolio Management, S. Chand & Co., 2004.

Black, F. and M. Scholes, "The Pricing of Options and Corporate Liabilities", *Journal of Political Economy*, 81 (May,1973), pp. 637-59.

Cox, John, Stephen Ross and Mark Rubinstein, "Option Pricing—A Simplified Approach", *Journal of Financial Economics*, 7 (October, 1979), pp. 229-64.

Gangadhar, V. and Dr. Mehari Tesfasus, "Management of Financial Derivatives", *The Chartered Accountant*, New Delhi, January, 2002, pp. 851-54.

Gardner, D.C., "Futures and Options", Indian Institute of Bankers, McMillan, New Delhi, 1999.

Mark, Rubinstein, "Derivative Asset Analysis", *Journal of Economic Perspectives* (1987), pp. 73-93.

Seth, A.K., International Financial Management, Galgotia Publishing Company, New Delhi, 2000.

Smith, C.W., "Option Pricing: A Review", *Journal of Financial Economics*, 3(1976), pp. 3-54 .

Thomas, Susan, "Derivatives Market in India", Tata Mcgraw Hill, New Delhi, 1998.

Vohra, N.D. and Bagri, B.R., *Futures and Options*, Tata McGraw Hill, Second Edition, 2003.

www.bseindia.com

www.nse-india.com

Exchange Traded Funds

An Innovative Financial Instrument

M.C. Garg and Deepti Gakhar

INTRODUCTION

Mutual funds have existed for decades, but ETFs are a relatively new and unique financial innovation. Index mutual funds democratized index investing in the 1970s by enabling small investors to combine their money and obtain economies of scale. Because of their orientation as low-cost investment vehicles, mutual funds limit active trading by only allowing trades once a day at the funds closing net asset value (NAV), as well as capping the number of trades as investor can make over a given period of time. These features make index mutual funds an unattractive option for institutions requiring liquidity and stock index futures contracts arose in the 1980's to meet this demand. By buying a futures contract to receive shares in the stock index at a given future date, institutions can recreate the performance of a stock index with a highly liquid security. Futures contracts are typically denominated in very high dollar values, so Exchange Traded Funds (ETFs) emerged in the 1990s to provide smaller investor with a way to buy and sell stock indexes throughout the day on the market.

EXCHANGE TRADED FUND : WHAT IS IT?

ETFs are basket of securities that are listed on an exchange and can be traded intraday. Investors can buy or sell shares in the collective performance of an entire stock or bond portfolio as a single security. ETFs are like equities as they trade on the open market and are like mutual funds as they encapsulate the performance of a basket of stocks. Neither equities nor mutual funds have fared well recently, and they are giving them both, a run for their money. The largest ETF, SPY currently has net assets of $28 billion. Yanguard Index 500, the largest of all mutual funds has $64 billion in net assets, buy it has an extra seventeen years of history behind it.

ETFs combine the attributes of a mutual fund with those of a stock. These are excellent cash products for average investors that offer them an entire range of index stocks as a package, without insisting on large investments. Investors can trade them throughout the trading day as in stocks. In comparisons in a traditional mutual fund, investors can purchase units only at the fund NAV, which is published at the end of each trading day. Consequently, the risk of price differential between the time of investment and time of trade is less in case of ETFs. A portfolio comprises of stocks that make up an index and tracks the specific index of which it is constituted. For example, Sensex Prudential ICICI Exchange Traded Fund (SPICE) is a fund that comprises of stocks contains 30-share BSE sensex and closely track the index.

History

The first ETF was launched in 1993 on American Stock Exchange (AMEX) and was called Standard & Poor's Depository Receipts (SPDR). SPDR tracks the S&P 500 index. Presently over 200 ETFs are listed on various stock exchanges globally.

Indian Scenario

India joined the club of developed market by launching Nifty Bees, the first exchange traded fund (ETF) from Benchmark Asset Management Company (BAMC). It was listed on the capital market segment of the National Stock Exchange on January 8, 2002. With this listing India has become the first emerging economy in Asia to launch an ETF. Prudential ICICI followed suit with an ETF named Sensex Prudential ICICI Exchange Traded Fund (SPICE) linked to the BSE Sensex. Actually the introduction of ETF in India was in hype for almost two years. The Bombay Stock Exchange in a joint effort with the Unit Trust of India had announced Sensex UTI Notional Depository Receipts (Sunders), the *desi* version of similar globally known funds like SPDRs, Webs, Diamonds and Cubes. However, due to some reasons, the proposed Sunders did not materialise.

Presently five ETFs are in existence in India.

- Sensex Prudential ICICI Exchange Traded Fund (SPICE)
- S&P CNX NIFTY UTI Notional Depository Receipt Scheme (UTI SUNDER)
- NIFTY Benchmark Exchange Traded Scheme (NIFTY BEES)
- JUNIOR BEES
- Liquid BEES

KEY FEATURES OF ETF

Following are the features of ETFs:

Buying and Selling Flexibility

Because they are exchange traded, ETF can be bought and sold at intraday market prices; purchased on margin; sold short, even on a down stick; traded using stop orders and limit orders, which allow investors to specify the price points at which they are willing to trade. In contrast mutual funds can be bought and sold at the close of trading.

Tax efficiency ETFs, like index funds in general, tend to offer greater tax benefits because they typically generate fewer capital gains than actively managed funds due to low turnover of the securities that compromise the portfolios. Generally, an ETF only sells securities to reflect changes in it's underlying index. Exchange trading of ETF further enhances their tax efficiency as investors who want to liquidate shares in an ETF simply sell them to other investors through exchange trading. Because of this feature, ETFs are not required to sell securities to meet investor cash redemption, potentially generating capital gains tax liability for remaining investors.

Lower Cost

Expenses have a significant impact on return for investors ETFs have other investment products. Since they are index-based, thus require few portfolio changes, resulting in much lower transaction costs than actively managed portfolios.

Diversification

ETF can cover sectors and indexes and thus provide diversification among groupings of large businesses, thus reducing the risk for investors of being vulnerable to price volatility in any one particular security.

Dividend Opportunities

Dividends paid by companies and interests paid by bonds held in an ETF are distributed to ETF holders, less expenses on a pro-rata basis. There may also be opportunities for reinvestment of distributions.

Transparency

To facilitate an ETF unique creation and redemption process, the composition file for each ETF creation unit is published daily. Since an ETF holdings are to provide performance similar to its underlying index, investors will essentially know the securities that are held in an ETF and their weightings.

Different Types of ETFs

ETFs can be categorized into three types of funds:

(a) Broad-Based—which tracks a broad group of stocks from different industries and market sectors. For example, i Shares S & P 500 index fund is a broad-

EXHIBIT I

Comparison between an ETF with a Mutual Fund and an Individual Stock

Attribute	*ETF*	*Index Mutual Fund*	*Individual Stock*
Diversification	Yes	Yes	No
Traded throughout the day	Yes	No	Yes
Can be bought on margin	Yes	No	Yes
Can be sold short	Yes	No	Yes
Tracks an index or sector	Yes	Yes	No
Tax efficient as turnover is low	Yes	Possibly	No
Low Expense Ratio	Yes	Sometimes	Not a factor
Trade at any brokerage firm	Yes	No	Yes

based ETF that tracks the S & P 500.

(b) Sector – which tracks companies represented in related industries.

(c) International – which tracks a group of stocks from a specific Country. For example, i Shares MSCI – Australia tracks the Margan Stanley Capital International index for Australian Stocks.

Mechanics of ETF

An ETF is created through an Initial Public Offering (IPO) by the asset management companies in which only authorised participants (AP), institutions such as Mutual funds companies, Insurance Companies and large investors are allowed to participate. These investors exchange their portfolio of stocks and a cash components for ETF also known as creation units. These creation units are made of two components namely portfolio deposits and cash components. Portfolio deposits consists of baskets of shares that make up an index and cash components which is the difference between the applicable NAV and the market value of the portfolio deposits. Cash components arises mainly due to transaction costs, rounding of shares and involvement of incidental expenses. These units can be either held as investment or sold in the market to the retail investors. They can be sold back to the issuer which buy it at a heavy

EXHIBIT II

Traditional Mutual Fund Structure

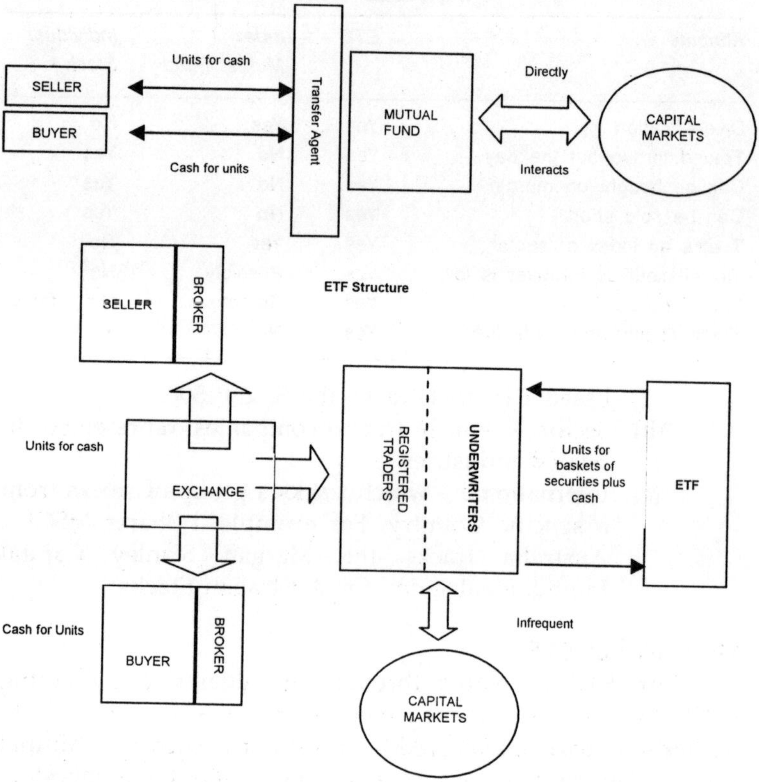

discount to encourage their selling on the exchanges. The net asset value (NAV) of an ETF is the value of the underlying components of the benchmark index held by the ETF, plus the accured dividend, less the accured management fee. ETFs do not necessarily trade at the NAV of their underlying holdings. Instead the market price of an ETF is determined by forces of supply and demand for the ETF shares. To a large extent, the supply and demand for ETF shares is driven by the underlying values of their portfolios, but other factors can also do effect their market prices. As a result, they could trade at a premium or at discount. And if ETF shares on the secondary market are over-priced or under-priced relative to the value of their underlying stocks arbitrageurs will step in. For example, if an ETF is traded at a discount to its net asset value, institutional investors could assemble share blocks in the open market at a discounted price, redeem them for the underlying stocks and sell those stocks at a profit. Thus, arbitrage opportunity would generate sufficient demand for the discounted ETFs shares to close the gap between their market price and the net asset value of their underlying portfolio. Exhibit III illustrates the same.

TO BUY ETF OR NOT TO BUY ETF

Why do Institutions use ETFs?

Cash Management

ETFs act as a short-term trading instrument. They can be used as a holding bay to park money, while the investor decides what to buy.

Managing Cash Flows

Investment manager who see regular inflows and outflows may use it because of their liquidity and their ability to represent the market.

Filling Gaps

ETFs tied to a sector or industry may be used to gain exposure to new and important sector. Such strategies can also be used to reduce an overweight or increase on underweight sector

Shorting or Hedging

Investor who have a negative view on a market segment or specific sector may want to establish a short position to capitalize on that view. Fund may be sold short against long stock holdings as a hedge against a decline in the market or specific sector.

Sector/country Equity Exposure

Exchange traded funds offer institutions immediate

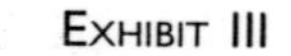

EXHIBIT III

ETF Share Creation and Redemption Process

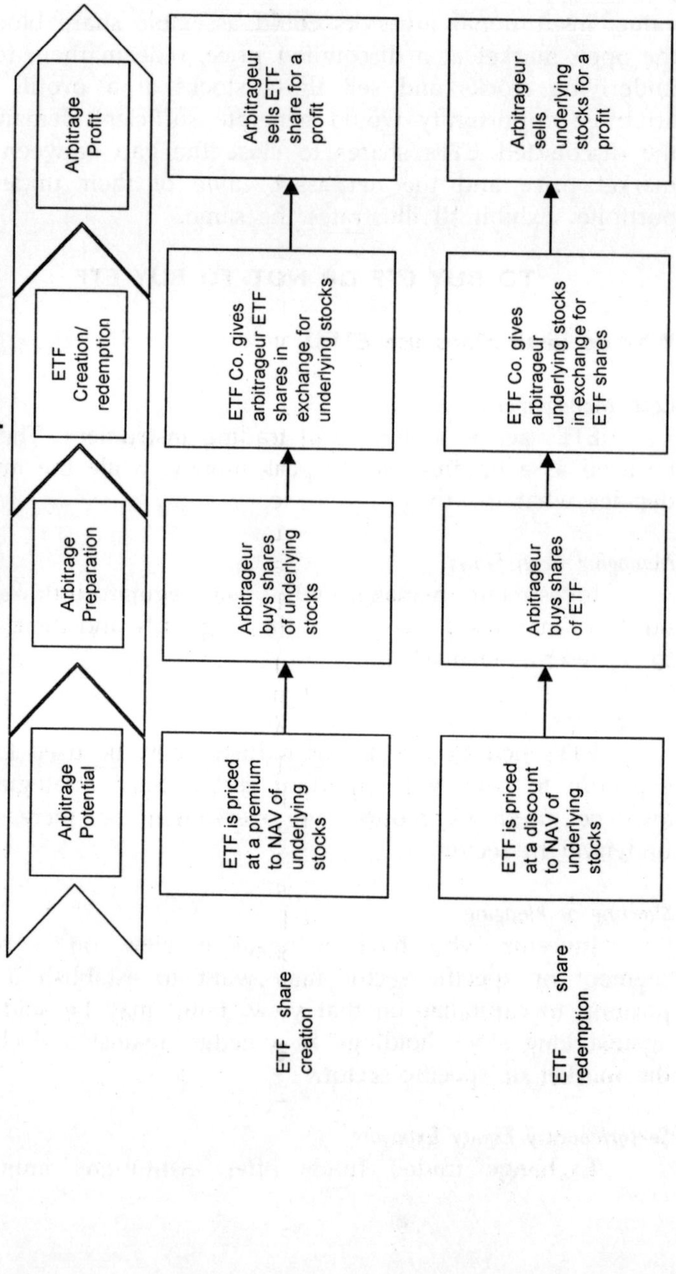

	Arbitrage Potential	Arbitrage Preparation	ETF Creation/ redemption	Arbitrage Profit
ETF share creation	ETF is priced at a premium to NAV of underlying stocks →	Arbitrageur buys shares of underlying stocks →	ETF Co. gives arbitrageur ETF shares in exchange for underlying stocks →	Arbitrageur sells ETF share for a profit
ETF share redemption	ETF is priced at a discount to NAV of underlying stocks →	Arbitrageur buys shares of ETF →	ETF Co. gives arbitrageur underlying stocks in exchange for ETF shares →	Arbitrageur sells underlying stocks for a profit

diversified exposure to a sector or country. For example, managers can quickly and easily purchase ETFs for instant and extensive international exposure, compared to the expense and difficulty of assembling a portfolio of foreign securities.

Disadvantage of ETFs?

- The expense advantage may prove to be more mirage than fact for most investors. Commissions like stocks, trading exchange traded funds will cost investors.
- Since they are traded on the open exchange, ETFs do not necessarily have to perfectly track the NAV of their holdings.
- Slippage as with stocks, there is a bid-ask spread, meaning one can buy it for 15-1/8 but can only sell it for 15 (which is a hidden charge).

Thus investing directly with a mutual fund company generally beats out ETFs in following situations:

- Non-taxable accounts.
- Small investments, i.e. if one invest a certain amount each month or are on some sort of automatic investment plan (ETF commission would kill investment.)

CONCLUSION

In recent years, unique features and benefits have helped exchange traded funds explode in popularity and emerge as one of the most flexible, multi-purpose investment vehicles available. But its just the beginning. ETFs deserve to be included in investor investment management tool kit. But investors should be cautious enough before they invest in units for several reasons. Cost advantage is not always as it might seem and their trading costs can quickly add up.

References

http://bseindia.com
http://benchmarkfunds.com
http://equitrend.com
http://institutional investor.com
http://ishares.com
http://investor.com
http://nseindia.com

Rasmussen Scott, "Going long with baskets : A cost-benefit comparison of exchange traded funds and index mutual funds". Honor theses, Stanford University, 2002 (http// econ.stanford.com)

Rive Steve, "ETF:A look under the Hood", October, 2003 (http://ishares.com)

5

Impact of FIIs on the Volatility of Share Prices

MANDEEP KAUR AND RENU SHARMA*

Global financial integration refers to financial liberalization and the increasing integration of the domestic financial market with the world financial markets. With the financial integration, developing countries have become increasingly attractive destinations for international investors who are seeking a higher return than what is available in the developed economies while diversifying their risk. Due to liberalization and economic reforms, Indian economy has moved towards rapid and sustained economic growth and globalization. As a result of this FIIs (foreign institutional investors) came into existence. For a developing country like India, opening up of stock market to FIIs can act as important role in improving efficiency of the market. In addition to this, arrival of FIIs is associated with the importation of technology, adaptation of the technology to the domestic environment and greater investments in improving information processing and financial services (Agarwal, 2000).

Foreign institutional investor has no lasting interest and basically is guided by considerations such as return, safety and liquidity of his investment. According to the RBI's criterion, FIIs investment includes the value of ordinary shares held by non-residents if such holding is less than 10% of total equity capital per investor. The value of preference shares, debentures and deposits of FIIs are treated as a part of the FIIs investment.

The FIIs currently operating in India are of different types. They comprise of pension funds, trusts, asset management companies and others. FIIs of different countries, predominantly American, began their operation in India (Cherunilam, 2003).

EMERGENCE OF FOREIGN INSTITUTIONAL INVESTORS

The foreign institutional investors have been allowed to invest in the Indian capital market since September 1992. The number of FIIs has increased from 1 in November 1992 to 517 in December 2003.

The 1990's began with major crises. In the wake of gulf war and the consequent expulsion of Indian expatriate labour from the Middle East, foreign exchange remittances fell down. As the balance of payments position deteriorated, a panicked withdrawal of funds deposited in India by 'Non-Resident-Indians'. As a part of the reforms agreed with the IMF, the rupee was devalued by 20%. The trade regime and the regulatory framework were liberalized and industrial licensing was abolished in all. Foreign direct investment was invited in a wide range of industries, including consumer goods. The government dropped its insistence that foreign equity participation provide specific benefits in terms of technology transfer or export earnings. The limit on foreign equity participation was raised to 51% for most industries and even 100% in some cases.

Foreign investment was especially sought in the infrastructure sector previously monopolized by state enterprises, i.e power generation, highway and port construction, telecommunications, oil and natural gas exploration, etc. and the services sector, where foreign capital had been gradually eliminated as a matter of deliberate policy was reopened to foreign investors. They were invited to invest in financial services, retail banking and recently in life and general insurance. Restrictions on the use of international brand names were removed. Reforms in the technology policy have provided greater recognition of intellectual property rights. This liberalization coincided with growing interest in emerging markets especially among the global pension funds. In a major break from the past, foreign institutional investors were allowed to make portfolio investments in Indian companies, subject to overall limits on ownership within each firm (Kumar, 2002).

REGULATORY FRAMEWORK

The regulations on foreign institutional investors, which were notified on Nov. 14, 1995, contain procedures of registration and general obligations and responsibilities of FIIs. According to the regulations, FIIs may invest only in:

(a) Securities in the primary and the secondary market including shares, debentures and warrants of companies listed on a recognized stock exchange in India; and
(b) Units of schemes floated by domestic mutual funds including Unit Trust of India, whether listed on a recognized stock exchange or not.

Joint ventures between a variety of domestic and foreign securities firms have been approved in the stock broking, merchant banking, assets management and other non-bank financial services sectors. The overall effect of FII investment and financial joint ventures has been the introduction of international practices and systems to the Indian securities industry. FIIs are permitted to invest in a company upto an aggregate of 24 percent of equity, which can be increased to 40 percent subject to approval by the Board of Directors and a Special Resolution of the General Body. In 1996-97, Government liberalized the FII investment policy, allowing them to invest in unlisted companies and corporate and government securities. FII investment has become an important determinant of the stock market trends in India (Cherunilam, 2003). Foreign Intuitional Investors can invest in India through two routes: Equity investment route and 100% Debt route. Under the equity investment, 100% investment could be in equity-related instruments or upto 30% could be invested in debt instruments, i.e 70% (Equity instruments) and 30% (Debt instruments). Under the 100% Debt route, 100% Investment has to be made in debt securities only (Chopra, 2003).

FOREIGN INSTITUTIONAL INVESTMENT IN INDIA: AN OVERVIEW

A major force that has changed the quantum and nature of international capital flows to India is the portfolio investment flows. India has witnessed a decade of portfolio flows and they are gaining more significance with every passing year. It has come to play a dominant role in the Indian economy. Portfolio investments include investments in American Depository Receipts (ADRs)/Global Depository Receipts (GDRs) and offshore funds in addition to investments by FIIs. Foreign portfolio investments in India have received importance and are allowed in the Indian stock markets as a follow-up of the recommendation of the Narasimham Committee report on financial system. The committee recommended their entry and stated that the capital market should be gradually opened up to foreign portfolio investments and simultaneously efforts should be initiated to improve the depth of the market by facilitating the issue of new types of equities and innovative debt instruments.

The Government of India issued the guidelines for FII investments on September 14, 1992. Prior to 1992, only Non-resident Indians (NRIs) and Overseas Corporate Bodies (OCBs) were allowed to undertake portfolio investment in India. Three years later in November 1995, Securities and Exchange Board of India (SEBI) notified the Foreign Institutional Investors' Regulations, which are largely based on the earlier guidelines issued in 1992. The country's stock market is opened up for direct participation by FIIs such as pension funds, mutual funds, investment trusts, asset management companies, nominee companies and

TABLE I

Composition of Foreign Portfolio Investment in India

(US $ million)

Year	*GDRs/ADRs*	*FII Investment*	*Offshore Funds*	*Total*
1992-93	240	1	3	244
1993-94	1520	1665	382	3567
1994-95	2082	1503	239	3824
1995-96	683	2009	56	2748
1996-97	1366	1926	20	3312
1997-98	645	979	204	1828
1998-99	270	-390	59	-61
1999-00	768	2135	123	3026
2000-01	831	1847	82	2760
2001-02	477	1505	39	2021

Source: Economic Survey, 2002-03.

incorporated institutional portfolio managers (Lakshmi, 2003).

Portfolio flows in India have become synonymous with FIIs investment. It is observed from Table 1 that the FII flows, which were only US $ 1 million in 1992-93, have risen over time and are at US $ 1505 million in 2001-02. The increasing proportion of FIIs in total portfolio investment shows their increasing role in foreign capital flows.

Table 2 shows an increasing trend of FIIs after their emergence. FIIs investments start increasing from 1992 onwards. However, the decrease in FIIs investments in Indian securities markets during 1994-95 was in line with the experience of other emerging markets, which also saw a decline in portfolio inflows. It further increased in 1995-96, this was because of greater diversification of Indian stock markets. The trend reversed in 1997-98 onwards because of nuclear testing at Pokhran. The developed countries imposed economic sanctions on the country. For instance, the US Exim bank had frozen all guarantees for capital goods exports to India. However, the trends in 1999-2000 and 2000-01 indicate a sharp increase reflecting improving external investors'

TABLE 2

Trends of FIIs Investment in India

(In Rs. Crores)

Year	*Gross Purchases*	*Gross Sales*	*Net Investment*	*Cumulative Net Investment*
1993-94	5592	466	5126	5126
1994-95	7631	2834	4796	9922
1995-96	9693	2751	6942	16864
1996-97	15457	6973	8484	25348
1997-98	16679	11803	4875	30223
1998-99	16114	17699	-1184	29039
1999-00	53716	43501	10218	39257
2000-01	70399	61697	9584	48841
2001-02	49962	41217	8746	57587
2002-03	46172	44186	2586	60173

Source: Centre of Monitoring Indian Economy, 2003.

sentiment as a result of improved global prospects.

There has been much work on the theoretical issues of FIIs like trends of FIIs in Indian companies (Kumar, *op. cit.*, 2003). Chakrabarti (2003) had analyzed the flows of FIIs and their relationship with other economic variables. It was concluded that these flows are highly correlated with equity returns in India and they are more likely to be the effect than the cause of these returns. Further the FIIs do not seem to be at an informational disadvantage in India as compared to the local investors. Aggarwal (1997) had studied the Determinants of Foreign Portfolio Investment in some Developing countries and their Macro-Economic Impact. Kishor (1997) had focused on the emerging role of FIIs in Indian Capital Market and concluded that FIIs investments greatly influence the share price movement but does not effect the equity market development of India. The present study shows the impact of FIIs on the Volatility of share prices.

Data Base and Methodology

The study is based on secondary information collected

from the various issues of economic survey, Centre of Monitoring Indian Economy (CMIE) and from the SEBI website. The data used to test the volatility of share prices comprises sensex observed at BSE and FIIs. The study covers the period from 1992-93 to 2000-01. Standard deviation and Co-efficient of variation has been computed to analyse the volatility in share prices and to calculate the standard deviation the following formulae have been used:

$$\sigma = \sqrt{\frac{\Sigma (x-\overline{x})^2}{N}}$$

where

σ = Standard deviation,

$\overline{x}$ = Average of share prices,

x = Monthly share prices observed at BSE sensex, and

N = No. of observations, i.e. 12 months.

To calculate coefficient of variation following formula has been used:

$$V = \frac{\sigma}{\overline{x}}$$

where

V = Co-efficient of variation

Volatility in Stock Market

Volatility has become a topic of enormous importance to almost anyone who is involved in the financial markets. To many among the general public, the term is simply synonymous with risk. High volatility is to be deplored, because it means that security values are not dependable and the capital markets are not functioning as well as they should. The capital market reforms since 1992-93 has contributed to a large extent in boosting the size and liquidity in the capital market. There were further infrastructure improvements in the stock market like introduction of screen-based on-line trading system by several stock exchanges, i.e. NSE (National Stock Exchange), BSE (Bombay Stock Exchange) and NSCC (National Securities Clearing Corporation). On the other hand, investments by FIIs since

TABLE 3

Monthly Averages of BSE Sensex

Years	Months											
	Apr.	May	Jun.	Jul.	Aug.	Sep.	Oct.	Nov.	Dec.	Jan.	Feb.	Mar.
1992-93	4131.01	3366.55	3088.59	2797.27	2829.96	3243.19	3075.28	2618.2	2535.64	2532.86	2708.72	2398.27
1993-94	2205.37	2248.01	2281.95	2190.34	2556.16	2708.39	2688.51	2850.35	3301.85	3813.74	4039.42	3811.25
1994-95	3824.75	3756.1	4135.67	4106.95	4407.4	4511.34	4351.16	4139.06	3949.78	3651.59	3474.92	3408.29
1995-96	3359.29	3206.86	3336.46	3334.86	3402.81	3396.37	3528.1	3172.02	3060.05	2979.3	3405.56	3327.33
1996-97	3599.66	3732.2	3906.72	3668.21	3449.17	3390.11	3159.79	3044.28	2918.68	3410.3	3453.24	3762.52
1997-98	3681.5	3740.95	4001.47	4256.11	4276.31	3944.79	3991.75	3611.83	3515.54	3472.87	3413.49	3816.87
1998-99	4006.81	3686.39	3250.69	3211.31	2933.85	3102.0	2812.49	2810.66	3055.41	3315.57	3214.62	3521.45
1999-2000	3325.69	3963.59	4140.73	4542.34	4898.21	4764.42	4444.56	4622.21	5005.82	5205.39	5320.51	5434.31
2000-01	4905	4253	4675	4647	4331	4417.0	3820	3928	4081	4152	4624	5421

Source: Compiled from various issues of Economic Survey.

1992 have affected the stock market behaviour and increased the volatility of asset prices at least in the short-run. The Table 3 indicates the monthly averages of share prices observed at BSE Sensex.

INVESTMENTS BY FIIs AND VOLATILITY OF SHARE PRICES

FIIs continue to play a significant role in share markets in India. As a part of liberalization process, foreign portfolio investment by foreign institutional investors has also been allowed. In fact, FIIs investment has so far vastly outpaced FDI inflows. Share prices in India have been influenced by the behaviour of FIIs. The opening up of the stock market to FIIs investment in 1992-93 led to a surge of FIIs inflows. This represented a diversification of the portfolio international investors into India, one of the emerging markets. The annual impact of FIIs on the volatility of asset prices is shown in Table 4.

TABLE 4

FIIs Investments and Volatility in BSE Sensex Index

Years	*FIIs Investments (US $ million)*	*Averages*	*Standard Deviation*	*Co-efficient of variation*
1992-93	1	2994	480.9	16.06
1993-94	1665	2891	682.2	23.59
1994-95	1503	3976	360.9	9.07
1995-96	2009	3292	158.0	4.79
1996-97	1926	3458	300.2	8.67
1997-98	976	3810	289.5	7.59
1998-99	-390	2909	355.1	12.20
1999-2000	2135	4339	611.4	14.08
2000-01	1847	4438	448.8	10.11

The above table also shows the FIIs investments, averages of share prices on stock market based on BSE sensex and the variation in share prices depicted through standard deviation and co-efficient of variation. Annual averages based on monthly share prices have been computed. Volatility of share prices is found to have declined after the arrival of FIIs until 1997-98 as the coefficient of variation starts decreasing. It started rising again since 1998-99, this is because of an immense decrease in FIIs during this period, but this was for a very short period. Volatility further decreased in 2000-01, so it can be said that volatility of Indian stock market has reduced after the arrival of FIIs.

However, the reduction of volatility can not be completely attributed to FIIs, it can be noted that the reforms in capital market like screen-based trading, dematerialization of shares and rolling settlements has yielded results and market become less volatile.

CONCLUSION

The stock market is increasingly becoming more centralized, concentrated and non-competitive. The FIIs have been playing an important role in this aspect. Volatility of share prices is found to have declined after the arrival of FIIs until 1997-98. It started rising again since 1998-99, this is because of decrease in FIIs during this period. Consequently, the ordinary investors have suffered heavy losses and lost interest in stock market. So the investments by FIIs should be reduced. This seems possible only by increasing the domestic investors' base (industrial and corporate) and encouraging mutual funds contracting the profit taking activities of FIIs. But even after the SEBI had provided operational freedom for mutual funds, the investor is not showing enough interest in mutual funds. In brief, it can be said that the volatility of Indian stock market has reduced after the arrival of FIIs. However, the reduction of volatility can not be completely attributed to FIIs, it can be noted that the reforms in capital market like screen-based trading, dematerialization of shares and rolling settlements have yielded results and market became less volatile.

REFERENCES

Aggarwal, R.N., (1997), "Foreign Portfolio Investment in Some Developing Countries: a Study of Determinants and Macro-Economic Impact", *Indian Economic Review*, Vol. 32, pp. 217-19.

Agarwal, R.N., (2000), "Financial Integration and Capital Market in Developing Countries", *Working Papers,* Institute of Economic Growth, Delhi University.

Chakarbarti, R., (2003) "FII Flows to India: Nature and Causes", http://www.prism.gatech.edu/rc/66/FII%20flows india.

Cherunilam, F., (2003) "International Investments", *Business Environments,* Himalaya Publications, pp. 608-09.

Chopra, C., (2003) "Foreign Institutional Investors and Stock Market Development in India", *Foreign Investment in India,* Deep and Deep Publications, pp. 212-22.

Economic Intelligence, Centre of Monitoring Indian Economy (CMIE), 2003.

Government of India, Ministry of Finance, *Economic Survey* of 1995-96, 1996-97, 1998-99, 1999-2000, 2000-01, 2001-02 and 2002-03.

Hooda, R.P., (2003), "Dispersion: It's Measures", *Introduction to Statistics,* Macmillian India Ltd.

Kishor, C., (1997), "Emerging Equity Market in India: Role of Foreign Institutional Investors", *Economic and Political Weekly,* Vol. 32, pp. 2729-32.

Kumar, S.S.S., (2002), "Foreign Institutional Investments: Stabilizing or Destabilizing", *Abhigyan,* Vol. 20, pp. 23-27.

Lakshmi, R., (2003), "FIIs Portfolio Investment Trends in Indian Companies", http://www.nse.india.com/content/press/may2003.

6

Foreign Institutional Investment in India

A Study of Issues, Facts and Determinants

Rohit Saini

I. INTRODUCTION

The recent wave of globalisation has affected all spheres of economic life and financial markets are no exception. Capital markets all over the world are increasing in their global character. The changes have been particularly unprecedented with respect to economies of Asia and Latin Africa. Deregulation has become the new *mantra* of success with the developing world. Since 1980s many developing countries have been liberalizing the inflow of foreign capital. Indian capital market however joined the suit in early nineties only. In 1991, compelled by the balance of payment crises, the government embraced Structural Adjustment Program, which is broadly aimed at liberalising the economic regime in country. For achieving the said objective, reforms have been continuously struck in all the institutions including capital market. One of the most important reforms in this direction was to open the doors of capital market for direct participation by foreign institutional investors (FII) in

Oct. 1992. Since then the country has been receiving large amounts of portfolio investment. However, by nature FI investment is very volatile and concerns have been expressed by economists all over the world regarding its potential to destabilise a developing economy. In this context it becomes very important to study the nature and behaviour of institutional investment.

Present study is an attempt to explore various theoretical issues relating to FI investment, its growth in India and factors that affect its inflow. Rest of the paper is organized as follows. Next section discusses various theoretical issues relating to pros and cons of foreign institutional investment. Section three traces the growth of FI investment in India. Section four provides a preliminary enquiry into the possible determinants of FI investment. Section five sums up the study.

2. PORTFOLIO INVESTMENT: THEORETICAL ISSUES

With the on going globalisation the role of institutional investors in foreign capital flows has increased to a great extent. They are being regarded as kingpin of financial globalisation. But what are the possible gains for a developing country form foreign institutional investment. The developing counties generally have a chronic shortage of capital. The entry of FIIs is expected to bring that much needed capital. However, as most of the purchases by FIIs are on secondary market, their direct contribution to investment may not be very significant. Yet, FIIs contribute indirectly in a number of ways towards increasing capital formation in the host country. Increased participation of foreign investors increases the potentially available capital for investment and thus lowers the cost of capital. Further, purchases of FIIs give an upward thrust to domestic stock prices and thus increase the price-earning ratio of firms. Both these factors are expected to increase overall level of investment in an economy. Thus, FIIs can prove to be an important boost for capital formation.

Portfolio investment is also expected to improve the functioning of domestic stock exchange. The host country seeking foreign portfolio investment has to improve its trading and delivery system. Also, consistent and business friendly policies have to be followed in order to retain the confidence of foreign investors. Both these factors catalyse the development of domestic stock exchange, which will benefit the domestic investors as well (Rao, Murthi and Rangarajan, 1999). Further portfolio investors are known to have highly competent financial analysts. They have access to most advanced technology, best possible information and vast and global experience in investment business. Due to these qualities the entry of FIIs can substantially increase the allocative efficiency of domestic stock market.

However, increased activities of FIIs in developing countries can also have negative impacts. Since the 1996 Mexican crises and widespread Asian crises, many economists have questioned the wisdom of policy-makers in developing world in indiscriminately inviting portfolio flows. Institutional investments are highly volatile and even in case of small economic problem investors can destabilise the economy by making large and concerted withdrawals. Many possible reasons have been mentioned in literature for explaining the volatility of portfolio investment. A straight forward reasoning follows from the fact that institutional investors actually act as agents of principle fund owners. The later generally observe the performance of agent investors at a short notice, often on the basis of quarterly reports. Because of this FIIs face very short-term performance targets. So they do not afford to stick to a lose making position even for a short period and withdraw at the first sign of trouble. Further, as the fund owners can shift between agent investors in very short period, the later follow the performance and activities of each other very closely. When one agent withdraws from an economy realising the initial sign of trouble, the others also follow the suit. Thus, a small economic problem can be converted into an economic disaster due to the herding behaviour of FIIs.

Another problem with Portfolio investment is that it influences the domestic exchange rate and can cause its artificial appreciation. The inflow of foreign capital raises the demand for non-tradable goods, which results in appreciation of the real exchange rate. With a floating exchange rate regime and no central bank intervention, the appreciation will take place through nominal rate (Kohli, 2002).

Such an appreciation will certainly go against the domestic country, as it will reduce its trade competitive strength. Under a fixed exchange rate regime, the inflows will result in a rise in money supply leading to an increase in consumption demand, thus causing a higher level of inflation in the recipient country.

The net impact of foreign institutional investment in a country will depend upon the policy response of concerned authority regarding the problems posed by such investments. For example, the policy response of Indian authorities has been generally to avoid a nominal appreciation by rather allowing a gradual increase in inflation (Acharya, 1999).

3. FOREIGN INSTITUTIONAL INVESTMENT IN INDIA

In September 1992, the Government of India opened up the doors of country's stock market to direct participation by FIIs such as pension funds, mutual funds, investment trusts, assets management companies, etc. They are welcome to invest in all the securities traded in primary and secondary market including the equity and other instruments of companies.

To undertake the business activities, FIIs are required to obtain an initial registration with SEBI. In addition, they need to comply with certain foreign exchange regulations for which they need to file an application with SEBI addressed to RBI. RBI's general permission is obtained by SEBI before granting initial registration under the single window approach. Both the permissions are initially valid for 5 years and are renewable for similar periods.

Government has been gradually extending the scope of FII operations by permitting additional categories of inverters to operate, recognizing additional instruments in which they can invest and altering the maximum allowable individual and aggregate FII share in a company. The current status is that an FII or a sub-account can hold a maximum of 5 percent of total issued capital of a company. Further, until otherwise permitted, the share of all FIIs and sub-accounts in one company should not exceed 24 percent of paid up capital of a company. However, this ceiling does not include investments made by portfolio investors through direct investment approval process and through purchases of global depository receipts.

Since the opening up of capital market, the country has been attracting large amounts of FI investment. Till the end of 2002, cumulative net investment by FIIs has reached an impressive level of $ 12000 billion. Table 3.1 catches the trends in capital inflows into the country.

Table 1 shows that on the whole foreign investment has followed a consistent trend since early 90s. Net portfolio investment has been positive in all the years except 1997-98, in which there was a net outflow. In most of the years share of portfolio investment is more than direct investment, particularly in the initial year. One of the reasons for

TABLE I

Foreign Investment Flows in India under Different Categories

(US $ Billion)

Year	*Total Foreign Investment*	*Out of which Direct*	*Portfolio*	*Out of FII*	*Portfolio GDRs/ SDRs*	*4 as per-cent-age of 3*	*4 as per-cent-age of 1*	*3 as per-cent-age of 1*
	1	2	3	4	5	6	7	8
1992-93	559	315	244	1	240	0.40	0.17	43.6
1993-94	4153	586	3567	1165	1520	46.6	40.0	85.8
1994-95	5138	1314	3824	1503	2082	39.3	29.2	74.4
1995-96	4892	2144	2748	2009	683	73.1	41.0	56.1
1996-97	6133	2821	3312	1926	1366	58.1	31.4	54.0
1997-98	5385	3557	1828	979	645	53.5	18.1	33.9
1998-99	2401	2462	-61	-390	270	—	—	—
1999-2000	5181	2155	3026	2135	768	70.5	41.2	58.4
2000-01	5099	2339	2760	1847	837	66.9	36.2	54.12
2001-02	5925	3904	2021	1505	477	74.4	25.4	34.1

Source: Compiled from Economic Survey, 2002-03.

apparently faster growth of portfolio investment could be that while FDI procedures remained complicated and discretionary, investment via the financial route was much faster and simple (Kohli, 2001).

In most financial years portfolio investment constituted between 30 to 40 percent of total flows. This clearly reflects the importance of portfolio investment for Indian capital market. Further column 6 reveals that FIIs have been the prominent carriers of portfolio investment into the country.

4. DETERMINANTS OF FII INVESTMENT IN INDIA

Empirical literature points out to many factors which can influence the inflow of portfolio investment into a country. However most frequently listed variable in literature is return on the stock. A higher return in capital market will make investment more profitable, thus attracting greater inflows. Most of the studies conducted so far do point towards a close relation between stock return and FII investment (e.g. Aggarwal 1997; Chakarbarti, 2001, etc.). However, there has been a controversy regarding direction of causation between returns and FII investment. Given the huge level of investment, foreign investors could play the role of market makers and book their profits, i.e. they can buy financial assets when the prices are declining thereby jacking-up the asset prices and sell when the asset prices are increasing. (Gordon & Gupta, 2003). Chakarbarti, 2001 finds a regime shift in the direction of causation. Specifically he concludes that in pre-Asian crises period it was found that FII investment has a significant impact on equity return. However, in post-Asian crises period equity return was mainly responsible for changes in FI investment.

Figure 1 depicts the movement in net foreign investment and BSE sensitive index. Both the variables do seem to move together, although the trend somewhat weakens in the recent years. The direction in the relationship also looks like changing with period. In the initial period return seems to be chasing investment while the relation inverses in the later part. Anyway, the close relationship between the two is quite clear from the figure. However,

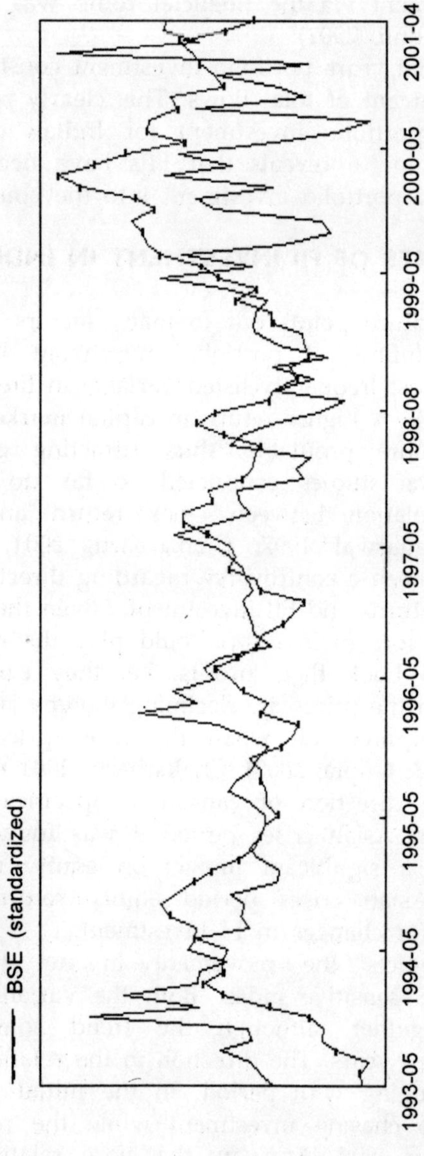
FII (standardized)
BSE (standardized)
1993-05
1994-05
1995-05
1996-05
1997-05
1998-08
1999-05
2000-05
2001-04

FIGURE 1

return is not the only factor explaining the movement in FI investment. Literature points out many other factors, which can influence FI investment. One factor that can certainly affect the flow of cross border capital flows is rate of exchange of domestic currency. When the exchange rate is higher, it will decrease the total earnings of foreign investors in terms of foreign currency, thus will discourage inflow of capital. However, higher exchange rate decreases the cost of stock for the foreign investor, thus providing an incentive to invest. The net impact will depend upon the relative strength of two factors. Another factor that can affect the inflow of capital is inflation rate in the recipient country. Specifically when domestic inflation increase, the purchasing power of invested funds decrease and hence investor is discouraged to invest in that country (Rai & Bhanumurti, 2003). In what follows an attempt is made to explore empirically the possible affect of these factors on FII investment in India.

4.1 Data and Variables

Data for present study mainly comes from 'Hand Book of Statistics on Indian Economy' published by RBI and latest issue of Economic Survey published by ministry of finance, Government of India. Although initially several variables were analysed, the finally fitted equation contains following four variables:

(i) Foreign institutional investment as a proportion of previous month's market capitalization of (FII).
(ii) Return on BSE sensitive stock price index (BSER).
(iii) Nominal effective exchange rate index based on 36 country bilateral weights published by RBI (NEER).
(iv) Inflation index based on wholesale price index derived as month-wise average of weeks (INFW).

Monthly data is used for all the variables. The sample consists of 73 observations for six years starting from January 1994 to January 2000. Many other data sets were also tried e.g. by adding the recent data, or discarding some previous data. The signs of all the independent variables remained consistent in all data sets, however the goodness of fit as well as significance of parameters was best with above sample. Therefore, some of the latest data was sacrificed in order to proceed with the most rebust results.

4.2 Empirical Methodology

First of all rate of return is calculated from BSE sensitive stock price index by taking the difference between log values of current and previous period, i.e.

$$R_t = \ln Vt - \ln Vt_{-1}$$

where R_t is return in period t, V_t and V_{t-1} are values of stock price index in period t and t-1 respectively.

Following regression equation is then estimated using ordinary least squares methodology (OLS):

$$FII_i = b_1 BSER_i + b_2 NEER_i + b_3 INFW_i + b_4 + U_i$$

where b_is are regression parameters and U is error term.

In order to check the direction of causality Granger's causality test is applied. There are many ways to implement a test of Granger causality. One particularly simple way consists of specifying autoregressive equations. We frame a null hypothesis that independent x variable does not Granger cause dependent y variable. Then firstly following unrestricted equation with p lags is estimated by using OLS:

$$x_1 = c_1 + \sum_{i=1}^{p} \alpha_i x_{1-i} + \sum_{i=1}^{p} \beta_i y_{1-i} + u_1$$

Where the null hypothesis is given as:

$$H_0 : \beta_1 = \beta_2 = ... = \beta_p = 0$$

Now following restricted equation is estimated also by OLS:

$$x_1 = c_1 + \sum_{i=1}^{p} \gamma_i x_{1-i} + e_1$$

An *F*-test of the null hypothesis is conducted by comparing the respective residual sum of squares, which are given as:

$$RSS_1 = \sum_{t=1}^{T} \hat{u}_1^2 \quad RSS_0 = \sum_{t=1}^{T} \hat{e}_1^2$$

If the test statistic given as:

$$S_1 = \frac{(RSS_0 - RSS_1)/p}{RSS_1/(T+2p-1)} \sim F_{p,T-2p-1}$$

is greater than the specified critical value, then the null hypothesis that *Y* does not Granger-cause *X* is rejected.

4.3 Results

Following is the estimated equation:

$$FII_i = .00720BSER_i + .00011NEER_i - .0006INFW_i - 1.948 + U_i$$

The regression results are summarised in Table 1 which show that both return variable as well as exchange rate variable are significant at 1 percent level. This shows that both return on stock and nominal exchange rate affects FII positively. As anticipated in theory, inflation variable has a negative sign suggesting that inflation in host country negatively affects the flow of FI investment into it. Overall fit of regression as judged from goodness of fit reveals that the explanatory variables explain about 30 percent of variation in FI investment.

However, significant regression parameters themselves does not predict the direction of causation between the dependent and independent variable. Therefore Granger's causality test is applied to know the direction of causation between the variables. Results show that the hypothesis that returns do not cause FI investment can be rejected at 1 percent level. Thus increased return on stock will favourably affect the inflow of capital. Further null hypothesis that inflation does not affect FII can be rejected at 1 percent level. Thus, a rise in inflation accordingly will set back the flow of institutional investment into the country. However, causation between exchange rate and FI investment could not be conclusively established.

TABLE 2

Regression Results, Sample Jan. 1994 to Jan. 2000, Total Observations 73

Variable	*Parameter*	*t-value*	*Inference*
BSER	.00720	4.064	Significant at 1 percent
NEER	.00011	2.790	Significant at 1 percent
INFW	-.00006	-1.830	Significant at 5 percent
CONSTANT	-.00322	-1.948	Significant at 5 percent
r^2	= .3139	Durbin-Watson	= 1.2305
Adjusted r^2	= .2901	Jarque-Bera	= 0.5207

TABLE 3

Results of Granger Causality Test

Null Hypothesis	*F-statistic*	*Inference*
Return does not Granger cause FII	3.565	Reject at 5 percent
FII does not Granger cause Return	0.801	Accept
Inflation does not Granger cause FII	4.939	Rejected at 1 percent
FII does not Granger cause inflation	0.852	Accept

Note: The test uses two lags.

5. SUMMERY AND CONCLUSIONS

The last two decades of twentieth century have witnessed the dismantling of controls on cross-border movements of capital in many developing countries. India also joined this category when in Oct. 1992 foreign institutional investors were allowed to invest in Indian capital market. Section two discusses the major theoretical issues regarding FI investment. The major arguments in favor of FI investment are its possible positive effect on overall level of investment in the economy and its contribution towards improvement in the functioning of domestic capital market. However intellectuals have raised the questions that possible negative impacts arising out of volatile nature of FI investment may over balance its benefits. The section concludes that net effect of FI investment on a country will mainly depend upon the policy response of authority to its possible negative implications. Section three traces the growth of FI investment in India. It is found that growth of FI investment has been quite consistent and impressive and particularly in initial years of reforms it has grown distinctively faster than direct investment.

In section four an attempt is made to explore the possible determinants of FI investment. Rate of return on stock as captured from the stock price index and domestic exchange rate have been found to affect FI investment positively while inflation in domestic country has a negative impact on it. Further from Granger's causality test it appears that FI investment is a result of return on stock rather than causing it. The causality tast between inflation and FI investment reveals that a higher inflation in domestic country causes retardation in flow of FI investment. However causality between rate of exchange and FI investment could not be confirmed.

References

Abraham, Joseph, Boosting Flow of Foreign Private Investment, *Yojana,* Vol. 38, No. 19, Oct. 31, 1994.

Agarwal, R.N. (1997); "Foreign Portfolio Investment in Some Developing Countries: A study of Determinants and Macroeconomic Impact", *Indian Economic Review,* Vol. XXXIV, No. 2, pp. 217-29.

Chakrabarti, Rajesh (2001), "FII Flows to India: Nature and Causes", *Money and Finance,* Vol. 12, Issue 7, Oct.–Dec.

Chandra, Vandana and Khan, M. Ali, Foreign Investment in the Presence of an Informal Sector, *Economica,* Vol. 60, No. 237, February 1993.

Choe, Hyuk, Bong-Chan Kho and Rene M. Stulz, 1999, Do Foreign Investors Destabilize Stock Markets? The Korean Experience in 1997, *Journal of Financial Economics,* Vol. 54, pp. 227-64.

Dyal, Ajit, Flow of Foreign Investments from Institutional Investors—Open Sesame, *The Economic Times,* Sept. 21, 1992.

Gordon, James and Poonam Gupta (2003), "Portfolio Flows into India: Do Domestic Fundamentals Matter?", *IMF Working Paper* Number WP/ 03/02.

Gupta, S.L., Foreign Direct Investment in India—An Evaluation of its Potential and Motive Consideration, *Finance India,* Vol. VIII, No. 2, June 1994, pp. 327-41.

Kohli, Renu (2001), "Capital Flows and their Macro-Economic Effects in

India", NCRIER, *Working Paper* No. 64.

Mani, Sunil, New Industrial Policy: Barriers to Entry Foreign Investment and Privatization, *Economic and Political Weekly*, Vol. XXVII, No. 35, Aug. 29, 1992.

Patnaik, Umesh C., Globalisation and Foreign Investment in India, *The Indian Journal of Commerce*, Vol. XLVI, Part IV, No. 177, Dec. 1993.

Pal, Parthapratim (1998); "Foreign Portfolio Investment in Indian Equity Markets, Has the Economy Benefited?", *Economic and Political Weekly*, March 14.

Pattanaik, Sitikantha and Bhaskar Chatterjee (2000), "Stock Returns and Volatility in India: An Empirical Puzzle?", *Reserve Bank of India Occasional Papers*, Vol. 21, No. 1. p. 18.

Rangarajan, C. (2000), Capital Flows: Another Look, *Economic and Political Weekly*, December 9, pp. 4421-27.

Samal, Kishore C. (1997), "Emerging Equity Market in India, Role of Foreign Institutional Investers", *Economic and Political Weekly*, Oct. 18.

7

Investor and Investment Education:
A Critique

K.V.S.S. Narayana Rao

INTRODUCTION

Individuals and institutions have an opportunity to invest as well as to do business in equity shares in stock markets. All individuals and institutions, which have long-term surplus funds, can invest in equity shares. But business opportunities will be limited and require greater effort, knowledge, skill, experience and organisation. Hence, every person or organisation cannot do business in shares profitably. Both investors and speculators/dealers (persons doing business in shares) have to evaluate the equity shares and make a judgment whether to invest or trade. The analytical techniques as well as the underlying assumptions that support the transactions are different between investment and trading. In this paper, the main hypothesis is that investment in equity shares was not given adequate coverage in investment texts. Taken to the extreme, it can be said that description of investment practice and analysis for investment was neglected in investment texts and the description of speculation/trading and its analysis was given prominence. If speculation dominates day-to-day stock market operations in many of the countries today, investment courses of universities may be the ones to be blamed. There are proponents of long-term investment in equity shares like Benjamin Graham[1,2], John Burr Williams[3] and Philip Fisher[4]. But the methods and the nature of the stock markets advocated by them were not communicated to the students and public in most of the investment texts. A number of investment texts are reviewed as a part of this study to bring out the perspective emphasized in them and to present evidence in support of the hypothesis.

The rest of the paper is organised as follows. In Section I, the nature of investment and business in shares is further explored. In Section II, the significant contributions of Graham, Williams and Fisher are outlined. In Section III, the hypothesis of the paper is presented. In Section IV, a review of investment texts is done. Limitations of the study are mentioned in Section V. We conclude in Section VI.

I. INVESTMENT AND BUSINESS IN SHARES

Corporate form of business organisation came into existence to pool the small amounts of capital available with large number of people into one big sum of money so that large ventures can be undertaken. When these ventures are of short-term nature, short-term savings of individuals are pooled together and the profits or losses of the venture are shared by the shareholders in proportion to the share capital contributed by them. Corporate form gives the advantage of limited liability. To set-up large factories to exploit the benefits of economies of scale in manufacturing, using the corporate form, long-term savings of people are to be pooled together to collect a large amount of share capital which is required to run the large manufacturing and distribution operation. The projects will normally have a long gestation period and investors have to wait for a significant amount of time to get cash dividends from the company. Individuals save and accumulate money to consume it at a later stage. The life cycle theory of savings assumes that individuals save during their working age and use it to consume during their retirement life. Hence, persons who buy shares of companies need to get back their investment at some point in time. Sometimes unforeseen liquidity needs may force individuals to sell the shares they purchased within a short holding period even though prices are not attractive. Stock markets came into existence to provide the service of exchange of outstanding equity shares between sellers and buyers. Stockbrokers, who function as members of the stock exchanges, can also participate in selling of equity shares to public by the companies.

Corporate concerns are set-up as organisations with perpetual life and investors cannot normally expect to get back the money they paid for acquiring the equity shares from the company. The companies normally invest the money in manufacturing and service facilities, which have technically a long life. Thus, the investment of companies is in long-duration assets. Simple asset-liability management thinking tells that long-duration assets are to be financed by long-maturity liabilities. This means, persons acquiring shares have to use long-term savings only. Any person who buys shares for investment purpose should not expect to get back the money in a short time with profit at the time he wants it. Therefore, at the time of buying shares, an analysis is to be done to determine whether it is rational to buy the shares at the existing market price from a long-term perspective. The long-term perspective is also called buy-and-hold perspective. In this perspective, the investor has to evaluate the profitability of the investment if he holds the investment up to the point of liquidation of the company. This perspective of investment and analysis is not discussed with sufficient detail in investment texts.

Stock markets create opportunities for business in shares. Broking is a simple example. Because individuals cannot spend a lot of time in the market waiting for the buyer to emerge, they employ brokers. It is also a normal practice in many asset and product markets for the broker to act as a dealer. A dealer purchases an asset or a product for his own account from the persons willing to sell it and in turn sells it to a buyer at a later stage. Dealers provide liquidity to the market. Similarly in the stock market also dealing services are required and number of persons act as dealers. The nature of the transactions in equity shares allows many individuals to act as dealers without a specific business location. Brokers facilitate dealing operations of individuals for commission. Brokers also solicit business from individuals who want to act as dealers as more number of transactions mean more commission for them. The nature of the trading transactions and the business interests of broking community combined to create a casino in stock markets. Stock markets provide a gambling opportunity for many with some intellectual involvement thrown in. Hence, a large number of books are written on trading. Magazines, radio and TV channels report on trading and give advice and lessons on trading to provide the intellectual support.

It is natural that descriptions of the practices in investment and trading/dealing/speculation are documented and scientific investigations are done on some of those practices to test whether they are fulfilling the objectives. Investment Management, Investment Analysis, Investments, Security Analysis, Portfolio Management are some of names under which the investment and trading in equity shares are taught in university courses.

Benjamin Graham, John Williams and Philip Fisher are proponents of long-term buy-and-hold investment in equity shares and they contributed significantly to the development of thinking to support investment in equity shares. Charles Dow[5] contributed significantly to popularise speculation (business) by the public at large.

II. CONTRIBUTION OF GRAHAM, WILLIAMS AND FISHER

Benjamin Graham taught a 2-hour course once a week at Columbia University from 1928 until his retirement in 1956[6]. He and David Dodd co-authored Security Analysis in 1934. They mention "the failure to properly distinguish between investment and speculation was in large measure responsible for the market excesses of 1928-29 and the calamities that ensued."[7] They attempted to distinguish between investment and speculation. The chief characteristics identified with investment by many authors at that time were: 1. Bonds, 2. Outright purchases, 3. Permanent holding,

4. Income, and 5. Safe securities. It is interesting to note points 3 and 4. These features still distinguish investment from speculation. At the time of purchasing if somebody comes to the conclusion that it is profitable to hold the security permanently and it will have an income at some point in time that gives him adequate return it is an investment decision. Graham and Dodd[8] define investment as "an investment operation is one which, upon thorough analysis, promises safety of principal and a satisfactory return." Operations not meeting these requirements are speculative. Analysis is the study of facts in the light of established standards of safety and value. The safety sought in the investment is protection against loss under all normal or reasonably likely conditions or variations. Benjamin Graham, in another book, Intelligent Investor, gave the standards of safety and value for defensive investors[9]. The defensive (or passive) investor is described as a person who will place his chief emphasis on the avoidance of serious mistakes or losses, and also wants freedom from effort, annoyance, and the need for making frequent decisions. This description fits anybody who has savings to commit to long-term investment. Graham discussed business in shares also in his books. Even this business in shares has to be supported by analysis and a concern for safety of capital. In section II.A, the standards specified for defensive investors by Graham are presented.

A. Standards for Safety and Value for Defensive Investors

1. Adequate Size of the Enterprise

The idea is to exclude small companies which may be subject to more than average vicissitudes especially in the industrial field. The size specified is $100 million of annual sales and above for an industrial company and $50 million of total assets and above for a public utility.

2. A Sufficiently Strong Financial Condition

For industrial companies current assets should be at least twice current liabilities. Also, long-term debt should not exceed the net current assets. For public utilities the debt should not exceed twice the stock equity at book value.

3. Earnings Stability

Some earnings have to be there for the common stock in each of the past ten years.

4. Dividend Record

Uninterrupted payments for at least the past 20 years.

5. Earnings Growth

A minimum increase of at least one-third in per-share earnings in the past ten years using three-year averages at the beginning and end.

6. Moderate Price/Earnings Ratio

Current price should not be more than 15 times average earnings of the past three years.

7. Moderate Ratio of Price to Assets

Current price should not be more than 1.5 times the book value last reported. However, a multiplier of earnings below 15 could justify a correspondingly higher multiplier of assets. As a rule the product of the multiplier times the ratio of price to book should not exceed 22.5.

We modified these standards to make them applicable to India as well as to incorporate some of the later ideas in valuation and made the valuation criterion unambiguous. These modified standards are presented in Section II.B.

B. Standards for Defensive Investors (Graham, Narayana Rao[10,11])

1. The company must have an adequate size. For Indian companies, Rs. 100 crore sales may be taken as adequate size.
2. The company must have strong financial condition. To satisfy this criterion, the current assets should be at least twice that of current liabilities and total debt-equity ratio should not be greater than 1:1.
3. The company must have paid dividends for the last

20 years. This may be modified to 10 years due to constraints of the databases.

4. The company must have earned profits for the last 10 years.
5. There should be earnings growth over the period of last 10 years. This condition may be specified as minimum growth of 10 percent per annum over the last 7 years in earnings per share (EPS). The idea is to buy companies whose growth in EPS over the last 7 years is equal to or more than the growth in the nominal GNP/GDP. The investor is to buy mature or growing companies.
6. Current price should not exceed 20 times of the average of the earnings per share of last seven years for companies with very good growth prospects (Companies having a growth of 20% and more per annum in EPS in the last 7 years). For companies having growth rate between 10% and 20%, the growth rate is to be the multiplier to be applied to the average EPS.
7. Current price should not be more than 1.5 times the book value last reported.

To do the analysis specified by Benjamin Graham investors require at least 10 years of financial statements. Even though it looks to be a straightforward numerical exercise to do these comparisons once data is available, in practice, it is a cumbersome exercise. Many MBA students are not able to complete the analysis of companies allotted to them. Hence, analysts are required to help the investors to identify the companies that satisfy these conditions as well as to refine the conditions for application to specific industries.

The value estimated by these standards is termed as intrinsic value and Graham recommends buying of leading issues (shares of companies that are leaders in their industry) at a price close to the intrinsic value (to the lower side). He advocates buying of secondary issues (shares of companies that have small market share in their industry) at a discount to the intrinsic value[12]. The argument being shares of secondary companies normally sell at a discount to the intrinsic value estimated by this method.

C. Contribution of Williams

Williams[13] began his book The Theory of Investment Value with the chapter on "The Difference Between Speculation and Investment." Williams defines an investor "as a buyer interested in dividends, or coupons and principal, and a speculator as a buyer interested in the resale price."[14] He went on to argue that rational men, when they buy stocks would never pay more than the present worth of the expected future dividends; nor could they pay less, assuming perfect competition, with all traders equally well informed. Such a price is the investment value of a security. Williams developed and advocated the dividend discount models. Investors are expected to buy below or close to the value given by the dividend discount models.

D. Philip Fisher's Analysis

Philip Fisher[15] recognizes that in the nineteenth and in the early part of the twentieth century, a number of big fortunes and many small ones were made largely by betting on the business cycle. In a period when an unstable banking system caused recurring boom and bust, buying stocks in bad times and selling them in good times had strong elements of value. This was particularly true for those with financial connections who might have some advance information about when the banking system was becoming a bit strained. He argued that establishment of Federal Reserve System and the measures taken to regulate the market after the depression reduced the opportunities for betting on business cycles. Fisher advocates finding the really outstanding companies and staying with them through all the fluctuations of a gyrating market. He listed 15 questions of qualitative nature to identify outstanding companies. The interesting point that he made is regarding selling the current holdings. According to Fisher, once a stock has been properly selected and has borne the test of time, it is only occasionally that there is any reason for selling it at all. Opportunities for attractive investment are extremely hard to find. Hence once an attractive investment opportunity is found after careful analysis, investors should not think of selling unless something extraordinary happens that threatens the well being of the company.

E. Contributions of Graham, Williams and Fisher—A Review

The common theme of Graham, Williams and Fisher is long-term buy-and-hold investment in equity shares. It is difficult to find equity shares that satisfy the standard of safety, quality and value and once an investor finds them he must stay with them for long periods of time. In contrast, speculators feel opportunities abound for making money. Day traders feel there are opportunities during the course of every day. There are differences in the thinking of these three authors. Graham emphasizes past performance and decision-making based on past performance only. Williams' model is based on forecasts of the future, but utilises past information also for estimating future. The model permits a forecast of future that can be different from the past performance. Graham will not approve it. Fisher concentrates on operational aspects and assessment of functional superiority and excellence of companies to make judgment regarding investments.

III. HYPOTHESIS

Investment texts did not cover the ideas of Graham, Williams and Fisher on investment and investment analysis in the right context. They gave more emphasis to analytical methods that advocated speculation/dealing/trading.

IV. REVIEW OF INVESTMENT TEXTS

It is interesting to mention that Benjamin Graham was appreciated in a number of investment texts for his contribution to the discipline of Security Analysis. But adequate description of the analytical methods that he advocated for equity shares is missing from in the books. In the case of Williams' Models, dividend discount models are the mainstays of Corporate Finance texts as well as Investment texts. But the discussion in most of the texts ends with negative comments regarding the method. Most of the authors conclude that it is difficult to provide the estimates needed to make the model work. Instead of devoting space in the investment analysis books to the methods that provide estimates, the authors conclude that dividend discount models are difficult to use in practice even though elegant and rational in theory. Providing estimates required by valuation models is also the job of the investment analyst. But most of the texts ignore this aspect to a large extent. The result is that there is a dearth of specialised books that concentrate on forecasting company financials from investment analysis perspective. Fisher is ignored altogether by authors of academic texts.

A. Appreciation of Benjamin Graham

Troughton[16] gives credit to Graham and Williams with the statement, "Taken together, Graham and Dodd and John Burr Williams provided the equity analyst with the framework to begin the mundane practice of determining what a stock would be worth to a rational investor." Burton Malkiel[17] says, "The firm-foundation theory is not confined to economist's alone. Thanks to a very influential book, Graham and Dodd's *Security Analysis,* a whole generation of Wall Street security analysts was converted to the fold."

Bodie *et al.*[18] pay a glowing tribute, "No presentation of fundamental security analysis would be complete without a discussion of the ideas of Benjamin Graham, the greatest of the investment "gurus." Until the evolution of modern portfolio theory in the latter half of this century, Graham was the single most important thinker, writer, and teacher in the field of investment analysis. His influence on investment professionals remains very strong." Francis[19] gave Graham and Dodd's book as a reference with the comment "This non-mathematical book is used by most fundamental analysts; it should be read by anyone who aspires to be a fundamental analyst." Wright[20] appreciates, "Graham & Dodd's Security Analysis became a classic through its pioneering contributions to investment analysis." Fuller and Farrell's[21] comment is, "For many years the process of security analysis was almost synonymous with what is now the generic term "Graham and

Dodd." "During the post-World War II period a popular text by Graham, Dodd, and Cottle became the "bible" for security analysts" is the comment of Curley and Bear[22].

White *et al.*[23] state, "the teachings of Graham and Dodd reigned supreme in the academic and professional finance communities. In their world, stocks have intrinsic value and investors could use ratios and other financial analysis techniques based on financial statement data to develop filter rules that identify stocks as over- or undervalued."

Despite these tributes, none of the books reviewed in this paper describe and criticize the analytical methods proposed by Graham in any detail. There is no example of successful application of the methods. Neither there are examples of unsuccessful application. The methods are simply ignored. Hence, the professionals who studied the currently popular textbooks on Investment Analysis and Security Analysis and learned investments theory would not even know what were the methods of Graham unless some of them tried to read the original books. The books of Graham are so voluminous and contain critical evaluation of a number of current practices of the day that a casual reader will find it difficult to grasp the message.

In contrast, investment texts discuss speculation on the business cycle in detail over a number of chapters and also discuss technical analysis in a separate chapter. In Section B the importance given to the coverage of E-I-C approach (also termed as top-down approach) and some of the negative comments on the dividend discount models (DDMs) in various investment texts are presented.

B. Negative Comments on DDMs and Positive Comments on P/E Ratio Models and E-I-C Approach

It is interesting to mention that there are two points of view even among academics regarding the objective of fundamental analysis. Some authors view fundamental analysis as a technique that gives value estimates for equity shares. The market price may coincide with fundamental value at some point of time in the future. Even if it does not coincide, the long-term investor will get his expected return through cash dividends. Within this school of thought, there is a subset whose thinking is market prices and intrinsic value coincide more frequently say every three or four years. Thus, according to this thought, shares can be bought when they are undervalued according to valuation formulas and held for three or four years to get a speculative profit through appreciation in the share price.

Another section of authors view fundamental analysis as a method that predicts market prices or explains market prices. In the works of these authors value and price are used interchangeably. Justified P/E ratios are obtained from the recent market history and it is assumed that indicated value or price target derived using information from the market history of P/E ratios would be attained in shorter periods of time. The usual time period assumed is 12 months. The existence of these counter-views creates some confusion in discussions when the two parties to a discussion are presenting their viewpoints with totally different interpretations of fundamental analysis itself.

Cohen, Zinbarg, and Zeikel's[24] comment is that the assumptions underlying the dividend discount model are so heroic that analysts have difficult in applying this technique to individual stocks. Francis[25] wrote that most common stock analysts prepare their estimates of intrinsic value per share by multiplying the stock's normalized earnings per share times the share's earning multiplier. It is further supported by the statement "For short-term forecasts (for example, 1 year or less in the future), a firm's earnings may usually be estimated from discussions with the firm's management and the firm's competitors, from publicly available information, and from other more-or-less subjective sources."[26] This statement by Cunnigham and Kolb[27] puts forward the view that fundamental analysis is explaining price, "Fundamental analysts believe that there is important information about the future course of stock prices contained in the fundamental or basics of the firm. Fundamental analysis uses all publicly available information about a firm in its attempt to predict the future course of a security's price." They also mention that a relatively straightforward technique for gauging the true value of a share of stock is the Fundamental Analyst's Model, which simply states that the true value of a share of stock equals the expected earnings for the firm in the next period, multiplied by justified P/E ratio for the firm's shares.

The problem with popularising one period's earnings as a valuation base is that when earnings suddenly dip, value estimates dip as P/E ratios are expected to remain constant in the short-run. In contrast, Graham advocates averages so that the effect on value is muted due to a bad year.

Reilly[28] argued in favour of top-down approach to analysing equity shares. Economy needs to be analysed first. In all texts that advocate analysis of economy, the discussion finally refers indicator analysis, which tries to identify business cycles. In no text, any economic analysis technique is mentioned or discussed that helps an analyst in arriving at estimates to use in dividend discount models. Dividend discount models require estimates of dividend growth for infinite periods and hence they require estimates of GNP growth for infinite periods, if as hypothesized, economy, industry and company performances are strongly interlinked. Speculating on business cycle is further supported by Reilly[29] with the statements, "If the economic outlook indicates a recession that will have an impact on all industries and all companies, it must be expected that all security prices will also be affected. Under such economic conditions, an analyst will probably be extremely apprehensive about recommending any industry."

In a latter edition Reilly and Brown[30] mention that there are two general approaches to the valuation process: (1) the top-down, three-step approach; or (2) the bottom-up, stock valuation, stock picking approach. Both these approaches have numerous supporters, and advocates of both approaches have been quite successful. Their vote is in favour of the top-down, three-step approach because of its logic and empirical support. So even though in this edition, they describe the dividend discount model and other discounted cash flow models in detail their support is still for E-I-C approach, which is an approach consistent with viewing fundamental analysis as a method of explaining stock prices over short periods. Another point of interest is that in this book, Reilly and Brown mention "Buy and hold", and "Indexing" as passive portfolio management strategies but discuss only indexing in more detail. Active investment strategies are also discussed in further detail but the "buy and hold" strategy does not have any further discussion. If "buy and hold" has to be the fundamental basis of investing in equity shares as this paper argues, such ignoring of the strategy in an important text used in CFA curriculum by Association of Investment Management and Research (AIMR, USA) is a major omission.

Fuller and Farrell[31] support the view of price estimation as the aim of fundamental analysis with the statements, "Security analysis involves the process of estimating the future cash flows which will accrue to the owners of a particular security, and the risk associated with these prospective cash flows. Generally the analyst's job also includes the task of estimating, either explicitly implicitly, the future price of the security." Fuller and Farrell[32] also talk good things about P/E models with the statement, "Traditionally, investors have utilized price/earnings ratio (P/E) models more than dividend discount models, although the latter have been gaining more and more popularity in recent years." Fuller and Farrell are to be given credit for pointing out that investors should not ignore the stock selection criteria proposed by Benjamin Graham in the many editions of The Intelligent Investor. The standards specified for defensive investors in various editions of the book by Benjamin Graham were given in a table. But still the description is insufficient because there is no application of the method and also there are no additional references to examples of the application of method by other authors.

"Historically, the stock market and the economy have been intertwined. Most stock market analysts agree that the stock market usually leads economic activity by six to nine months, but once in gear, the economy drives corporate earnings and dividends, which, in turn impact stock values." This is the statement of Hirt and Block.[33]

Gitman and Joenk[34] clearly describe the role of buy-and-hold strategy: "This is the most basic and certainly one of the most conservative of all investment strategies; the objective is to place money in a secure investment outlet (safety of principal is vital) and watch it grow over time.

High-quality stocks that offer attractive current income and/or capital gains are selected and held for extended periods—perhaps as long as 15 or 20 years. This type of strategy is often used to finance future retirement plans, to meet educational requirements, or simply as a convenient way of accumulating capital over long haul. The buy-and-hold strategy minimizes the amount of time an investor must devote to portfolio management. Risk is also kept low; most buy-and-hold investors are conservative, quality-conscious individuals who are satisfied with more modest rate of return over long haul." Despite this clear description of the buy-and-hold strategy there is no explicit discussion of analysis to be done by investors or their advisors to select stocks for buy-and-hold investment in this book. Instead, traditional security analysis is described as the "top-down" approach that begins with economic analysis, then moves to industry analysis, and finally to fundamental analysis. Fundamental analysis rests on the belief that the value of a stock is influenced by the performance of the company that issued the stock. If company prospects look strong; the market price of the stock would reflect that and be bid up. Thus, the reader has the description of business cycle related analysis of security prices. Most of the books in investment field describe in detail the E-I-C approach, which as mentioned repeatedly is betting on business cycle.

Mitra and Gassen[35] have a similar view. They wrote that Studies had shown that security price changes were related to concurrent changes in the market and the market acts as a surrogate for the economy as well as for the various groups of industries.

Jones[36] writes, "The P/E ratio or earnings multiplier approach is the best known and most widely used valuation technique. Analysts are more comfortable talking about EPS and P/E ratios, and this is how their reports are often couched. This is the typical language of Wall Street." A typical criticism of dividend discount model can be seen in Jones' book[37]. "In theory, the discounted cash-flow approach is a correct, logical, and sound position. Consequently, the best estimate of the current value of a company's common stock is the present value of the (estimated) cash flows to be generated by that company. However, some analysts and investors feel that this model is unrealistic. After all, they argue, with regard to the DDM no one can forecast dividends into the distant future with very much accuracy. Technically, the model calls for an estimate of all dividends from now to infinity, which is an impossible task. Finally, many investors want capital gains and not dividends, so for some investors focusing solely on dividends is not desirable."

Sharpe *et al.*[38] mention in their introduction to the chapter on "The Valuation of Common Stocks" that one purpose of financial analysis is to identify mispriced securities. Security analysts estimate the firm's future earnings and dividends and if these estimates are substantially different from the average estimates of other analysts, they identify an instance of mispricing. If it is also felt that the market price of the security will adjust to reflect these more accurate estimates, the analyst will issue either a buy or sell recommendation. Thus, the introduction itself starts with the perspective of business in shares. The investment perspective is not brought out. However, they described in an appendix, the Graham-Rea model of identifying mispriced securities for active investment and also brought out the fact that Graham supported efficient markets hypothesis.[39]

Fischer and Jordan[40] focused only on a one-year horizon throughout their book with the argument that even in the true investment situation, the investor or analyst must constantly review each security's performance relative to the market over short periods. A very interesting comment was made by Fischer and Jordan[41] in a passing manner at the conclusion of a chapter that traditional techniques using "normal" P/E ratios allow investors to evaluate a stock for a short-term horizon. An approach combining the dividend discount model can be helpful in evaluating a stock for a longer-term holding period. This statement comes too late in the book to make any impact on students or readers. This statement sums up the need for this paper. In majority of the investment texts, investment and speculation were not adequately distinguished. Even though methods of analysis for investment were proposed by some proponents, most of the textbook authors did not include them in their texts in right context and explanation. There is no advocacy for investment. Instead, there was a detailed explanation of techniques dealing with business cycle analysis and its impact on stock prices. These explanations further gave rise to one-year horizon analysis of stock prices and even analysis over much shorter periods.

V. LIMITATIONS OF THE STUDY

All the texts examined in this paper are published after 1975. This could be a limitation to strongly assert that any other author of investment texts did not promote Graham's methods. Janet Lowe[42] wrote a book titled "Value Investing Made Easy" in which she described the utility of Graham's ideas. She gave a recommended reading of books. There is no reference to any investment text apart from some of the books reviewed in this paper. That strengthens the argument Graham's methods based on past results were not supported by any subsequent textbook author.

VI. CONCLUSION

There is a strong need for change of orientation in investment texts. Analysis for investment and analysis for business in shares have to be described in separate chapters so that students and readers clearly understand the rationale of each of these types of analysis. A dealer who is concerned with order flow on a minute-to-minute basis may not be concerned that much with discounted cash flow analysis. He may try to employ tactics based on some short-term market factors. His analytical techniques are not useful to a person who comes to the stock market to invest for long-term. Rationally, a long-term investor should not touch any security that is selling above the DCF valuation. If the market goes above the rational values, investor need not worry about it except for the fact that he will not have an opportunity to place his funds in equities. It is not his job to enter into short-selling operations. He is not equipped to do such business operations and he has to leave such things to people who specialise in business operations in the markets. There is no doubt a need to discuss analytical techniques involved in business in equity shares in investment texts. But a clear distinction needs to be made between the two different activities in equity shares.

In this context, the emphasis is to be given to the idea of fair value investing. The current emphasis is on investing in bargains or undervalued securities. The investment texts should also contain chapters devoted to forecasting company fundamental information and even full length books need to be devoted to this aspects of security analysis. Because, analysis for investment was neglected in a number of investment texts, even research output on this activity is inadequate. More research was done on testing efficient markets hypothesis than on helping investors to take rational investment decisions, which only will make a market efficient even in theory.

At S.P. Jain Institute of Management and Research, Mumbai, a beginning is made in this direction through an all-India competition on Equity Research for business school students. The event has two categories—one recommendation for buy-and-hold investment and the other—recommendation for one-year horizon short-term trading. It is interesting to note there were more entries (around 40) for the long-term category in comparison to short-term (10) in the competition conducted in December 2003. Most of the long-term category entries used DCF techniques. But it was observed that estimation methods used were not to the satisfaction of many. That could be because of inadequate attention is given to estimating and forecasting in investment texts.

Notes and References

1. Graham, Benjamin and Dodd, David, 1934, Security Analysis, The Classic 1934 edition, McGraw Hill, New York.
2. Graham, Benjamin, 1973, The Intelligent Investor, 4th revised edition, Harperbusiness, New York, 1973
3. Williams, John Burr, 1938, The Theory of Investment Value, North-Holland Pub. Company, Amsterdam
4. Fisher, Philip A., 1996, Common Stocks and Uncommon Profits and other Writings, John Wiley & Sons, New York
5. Fischer, Donald E., and Jordan, Ronald J., 1995, Security Analysis and

Portfolio Management, 6th edition, Prentice-Hall Inc., Englewood Cliffs, N.J., p. 511.

6. Lowe, Janet, 1996, Value Investing Made Easy, The McGraw Hill Inc., New York.
7. Graham, Benjamin and Dodd, David, 1934, *op. cit.*, p. 50.
8. Graham, Benjamin and Dodd, David, 1934, *op. cit.*, P. 54.
9. Graham, Benjamin, 1973, *op. cit.*, pp. 184-86.
10. Narayana Rao, K.V.S.S., 2003, "Analysis for Investment and Speculation in Equity Shares," Presented in National Seminar on Emerging Trends in Financial Services and International Business, Department of Business Management, Guru Jambheshwar University, Hisar, March 24-25.
11. Narayana Rao, K.V.S.S., 2003, "A nine-step route to picking value stocks", Business Standard-Smart Investor, August 25.
12. Graham, Benjamin, 1973, *op. cit.*, p. 92.
13. Williams, John Burr, 1938, *op. cit.*
14. Williams, John Burr, 1938, The Theory of Investment Value, North-Holland Pub. Company, Amsterdam, p. 4.
15. Fisher, Philip A., 1996, *op. cit.*
16. Troughton, George H., 2002, Foreword to Stowe, John D., *et. al.*, Analysis of Equity Investments: Valuation, AIMR, Charlottesville, p. xiv.
17. Malkiel, Burton G., 1999, A Random Walk Down Wall Street, Revised Edition, W.W. Norton & Company, p. 30.
18. Bodie, Z. and Kane A., 1995, Essentials of Investments, Richard D. Irwin, Chicago, p. 373.
19. Francis, Jack Clark, 1986, Investments: Analysis and Management, Fourth edition, McGraw-Hill Book Company, New York, p. 453.
20. Wright, Leonard T., Principles of Investments: Text and Cases, Second Edition, Grid Inc., Columbus, Ohio, 1977, p. 4.
21. Fuller, Russell J. and Farrell, James L., 1987, Modern Investments and Security Analysis, McGraw-Hill Book Company, New York, p. 10.
22. Curley Anthony J. and Bear, Robert M., 1979, Investment Analysis and Management, Harper & Row, Publishers, New York, p. 167.
23. White, Gerald I., Sondhi, Ashwinpaul C., and Fried, Dov, 2003, The Analysis and Use of Financial Statements, Third Edition, John Wiley & Sons, Singapore, pp. 165-66.
24. Cohen, J.B., Zeikel, Arthur, and Zinbarg, E.D., 1977, Investment Analysis and Portfolio Management, Third Edition, Richard D. Irwin, Homewood, Illinois, p. 243.
25. Francis, Jack Clark, 1986, *op. cit.*
26. Francis, Jack Clark, 1986, *op. cit.*, p. 481.
27. Cunningham, Rosemary Thomas and Kolb, Robert W., 1993, Introduction to Investments, Kolb Publishing Company, Miami, Florida, p. 193.
28. Reilly, Frank K., 1979, Investment Analysis and Portfolio Management, The Dryden Press, Hinsdale, Illinois,

29. Reilly, Frank K., 1979, *op. cit.*, p. 227.
30. Reilly, Frank K., and Brown, Keith C., 2003 Investment Analysis and Portfolio Management, Seventh Edition, Thomson South-Western, First Reprint, Thomson Asia Pvt. Ltd., Singapore.
31. Fuller, Russell J. and Farrell, James L., 1987, *op. cit.*, p. 9.
32. Fuller, Russell J. and Farrell, James L., 1987, *op. cit.*, p. 361.
33. Hirt, Geoffrey A. and Block, Stanley B., 1999, Fundamentals of Investment Management, Irwin McGraw-Hill, Boston, p. 129.
34. Gitman, Lawrence J. and Joehnk, Michael D., 1984, Fundamentals of Investing, Second Edition, Haper & Row, Publishers, New York, p. 297.
35. Mittra, Sid and Gassen, Chris, 1981, Investment Management, Harcourt Brace Jovanovich, Inc., New York.
36. Jones, Charles P., 2002, Investments: Analysis and Management, John Wiley & Sons, Inc., New York, p. 268.
37. Jones, Charles P., 2002, *op. cit.*, p. 275.
38. Sharpe, William F., Alexander, Gordon J., and Bailey, Jeffrey V., 1995, Investments, Fifth Edition, Prentice-Hall, Inc., Englewood Cliffs, N.J.,
39. Sharpe, William F., Alexander, Gordon J., and Bailey, Jeffrey V., 1995, *op. cit.*, pp. 603-04.
40. Fischer, Donald E., and Jordan, Ronald J., 1995, *op cit.*
41. Fischer, Donald E., and Jordan, Ronald J., 1995, *op cit.*, p. 279.
42. Lowe, Janet, 1996, *op. cit.*

8

Liquidity and Returns after Dematerialisation

A Study of BSE Listed Companies

KARAMJEET KAUR

INTRODUCTION

The traditional scrip-based system has involved enormous paper work. The scrip-based system is very complex and time-consuming and is associated with many problems like fake certificates, tearing/mutilation of certificates, fake certificates in transit, signature differences, delays in postal transit, etc. Depository system offers scope for paperless trading. In depository system share certificates belonging to the investors are dematerialized and their names are entered in the records of the depository as beneficial owners.

Dematerialisation is the process by which investors' share certificates are taken back by the company through the Depository Participant, verified and if found in order, demat is confirmed by the company and then an equivalent number of shares are credited by the Depository Participant to investors' account as electronic holding. This process can be reversed at the desire of the investor.

Reverse process is called 'rematerialisation', where electronic holding of investors are converted back into share certificates in paper form. The demat process is to be completed within 15 days while remat is to be completed within 30 days. The institutions connected with demat operations include: (a) depository, (b) stock exchanges, (c) clearing corporations/clearing houses, (d) depository participants, (e) registrars, and (f) investors.

India has adopted multiple depository system and at present there are two depositories, i.e. NSDL and CDSL. The first scrip which was traded in demat form in India was that of Reliance industries on Nov. 29, 1996 on NSE. The Government of India introduced Depository Bill in Lok Sabha in July 1997 to start scrip less trading. (Bansal, Lalit K., 2001)

Dematerialisation of shares is associated with great benefits to the investors, to the issuers, to the intermediaries and to the country as a whole. Ownership transfer of demat shares is quite fast. It completely eliminates the risk of bad deliveries which in turn eliminate all costs and wastage of time associated with the follow up for rectification. This reduction in risk associated with bad delivery has led to reduction in brokerage to the extent of 0.5% by quite a few brokerage firms. Moreover, there is saving in stamp duty when shares are electronically transferred. Also, if share certificates are lost in transit, in case of scrip-based trading, or become mutilated or misplaced investors has to spend at least Rs. 500 for indemnity bond, newspaper advertisement, etc. which can be eliminated completely in the demat form. Investors can also get their bonuses and rights directly in their account.

Demat shares are definitely a superior product. This leads to enhanced liquidity which will enable investors to have access to greater reinvestment opportunities due to speedier transfer of funds and securities. As transfer process is quick, naturally there will be more demand for shares and this will increase increased traded volume, after demat. Higher demand is expected to push up prices of demat shares. The objective of this paper is to test this phenomenon that whether demats is associated with increased liquidity and higher returns to the investors. The rest of the paper is organized as: Section I discusses the relevant literature on this issue, Section II discusses data sources and selection criterion, Section III discusses the methodology, Section IV analyses the results, and Section V discusses the findings.

I. REVIEW OF LITERATURE

Raju, M.T. and Patil, Prabhakar R. (www.utiicm.com/prabhakar_patil.html) studied the impact of dematerialization on liquidity, returns and volatility of NSE listed 28 companies during the year 1999 by employing event study methodology and found the results very much favourable in the sense that dematerialization is associated with higher abnormal return, high liquidity and more volatility as compared to pre-demat period.

So far, this is the only study found in literature; hence the need is felt to study this phenomenon in other periods as well as in other stock exchanges.

II. DATA SOURCES AND SELECTION CRITERION

Sample consisted of 35 BSE listed companies for which compulsory demat was made effective from 17th January, 2000. The list for such companies has been taken from www.indiainfoline.com. In this list 40 companies were found but later on for 5 companies there was no trading during the relevant time under study. The list of such companies is annexed to this paper. The share prices and trading volumes of the companies have been taken from 'SAM' CD-ROM data base of BSE. The benchmark index representing the market portfolio is the BSE-Sensex.

III. RESEARCH METHODOLOGY

Returns

We take the null hypothesis that dematerialsation has no impact on the returns of the security and the alternative hypothesis is that the demat is associated with abnormal returns. To measure the abnormal returns, we have used "event study methodology" as used by Compbell, Lo and

Makinlay (1997) and by Raju and Patil.

The following steps are involved:

Daily abnormal returns for security 'i' for 100 trading days, starting from the date of compulsory demat have been calculated as:

$$AR_{it} = R_{it} - E\ (R_{it})$$

where

t = 0 to 100 trading days, if event day is taken as 0.

AR_{it} = Abnormal return on security 'i' for day 't'.

R_{it} = Raw return on security 'i' for day 't' which is calculated as:

$$R_{it} = \frac{MP_{i,\ t} - MP_{i,\ (t-1)}}{MP_{i,\ (t-1)}}$$

Where

$MP_{i,\ t}$ = Market Price of security 'i' on day 't'.

$MP_{i,\ (t-1)}$ = Market Price of security 'i' on day 't-1'

$E\ (R_{it})$ = Expected return on security 'i' during day 't' which is estimated using Capital Asset Pricing Model (CAPM).

$E\ (Rit)$ = $á_i + â_i R_{mt} + e_{it}$

where $á_i$ and $â_i$ are intercept and slope parameters and e_{it} is residuals of security i.

$\hat{A}_i$ = beta coefficient (measure of systematic risk of security i) which is calculated as

$$\hat{A}_i = \frac{Cov\ (R_i,\ R_m)}{ó_m^{\ 2}}$$

where

$Cov\ (R_i,\ R_m)$= Covariance between the return on security i and the return of market portfolio.

$ó_m^{\ 2}$ = Variance of return on market portfolio.

$á_i = R_i - â_i\ R_m$

R_i = Mean return of security i.

R_m = Mean return of portfolio m.

The stock returns have been regressed to BSE Sensex returns for a period of 120 trading days before the event under study.

The abnormal returns are then aggregated in order to compute CAR (Cumulative abnormal return) for each company.

To carry out the testing for the significance of abnormal returns, SCAR (Standardized Cumulative Abnormal Returns) have been calculated as:

$$SCAR = \frac{CAR_i}{\acute{o}_i}$$

Under the null hypothesis, the distribution of SCAR is student 't' with L-2 degrees of freedom, where L is the length of CAR. Here in this study, as we have taken 100 trading days, the distribution of SCAR will be well approximated by the standardized normal distribution.

Liquidity

If we assume that demat does not effect liquidity, there should be no growth in trading volumes after demat.

Trading volumes has been considered as the surrogate for liquidity. In order to measure the growth in the traded volumes in the post-demat period, growth rates have been calculated as follows:

$$G_i = \frac{Ty_i - Tx_i . 100}{Tx_i}$$

where

G_i = Growth in volumes of company i.

Ty_i = Total traded volumes during the post-demat period of company i.

Tx_i = Total traded volumes during pre-demat period of company i.

Traded volumes have been aggregated for 100 trading days for pre-demat as well as for post-demat period for each company.

IV. ANALYSIS AND INTERPRETATION

Abnormal Returns

TABLE I

Name of company	*CAR(%)*	*SCAR(%)*
Amara Raja Batteries Ltd.	-79.97	-18.93
Archies Greetings & Gifts Ltd.	-58.42	-13.46
Atlas Copco (India) Ltd.	-77.85	-18.88
Blue Star Ltd.	-291.4	-23.44
Carrier Aircon Ltd.	-14.65	-4.698
Electrosteel Castings Ltd.	-138.2	-27.05
Exide Industries Ltd.	-60.06	-16.56
German Remedies Ltd.	-39.67	-8.885
Gujarat Gas Company Ltd.	-68.52	-15.58
Gujarat State Fertilisers & Chemicals Ltd.	-27	-8.142
Himachal Futuristic Communications Ltd.	-84.56	-10.79
Hindustan Lever Chemicals Ltd.	-55.33	-16.19
Hindustan Motors Ltd.	-62.63	-9.376
Hoechst Marion Roussel Ltd.	-123.5	-26.61
ICI India Ltd.	-83.64	-22.38
Indian Oil Corporation Ltd.	-21.85	-5.992
Indian Shaving Products Ltd.	-88.2	-23.36
Ingersoll-Rand India Ltd.	-41.84	-10.37
Knoll Pharmaceuticals Ltd.	-20.99	-5.528
Madras Cements Ltd.	-41.56	-10.63
MRF Ltd.	-43.95	-10.16
Nicholas Piramal India Ltd.	-111.1	-25.71
Parke Davis (India) Ltd.	-41.7	-10.46
Punjab Tractors Ltd.	-0.874	-0.195*
SSI Ltd.	-134	-15.55
Supreme Industries Ltd.	-77.07	-19.93
Thomas Cook (India) Ltd.	-31.68	-5.736
Titan Industries Ltd.	-106.7	-27.34
Torrent Pharmaceuticals Ltd.	-286.9	-50.38
Trent Ltd.	-14.2	-3.065
Unichem Laboratories Ltd.	-160.9	-23.2
United Phosphorus Ltd.	-50.78	-11.04
Vatsa Corporation Ltd.	-326	-22.24
Videocon International Ltd.	-53.84	-10.9
Voltas Ltd.	-0.113	-0.028*

* denotes not significant.

As shown in Table 1, all the 35 companies are showing negative cumulative abnormal returns as well as standardized cumulative average returns, which are significant at 1% as well as 5% level of significance except 2 companies. Hence, we accept our null hypothesis that there are no positive abnormal returns associated with demats.

Trading Volumes

TABLE 2

Name of company	*Pre-demat traded volume*	*Post-demat traded volume*	*Growth (%)*
Amara Raja Batteries Ltd.	4485040	2170178	-51.61
Archies Greetings & Gifts Ltd.	434090	200751	-53.75
Atlas Copco (India) Ltd.	2352289	558653	-76.25
Blue Star Ltd.	2730887	1173245	-57.04
Carrier Aircon Ltd.	10787642	2718293	-74.8
Electrosteel Castings Ltd.	425488	85383	-79.93
Exide Industries Ltd.	2055979	1089800	-46.99
German Remedies Ltd.	2329625	1288092	-44.71
Gujarat Gas Company Ltd.	4801456	2318221	-51.72
Gujarat State Fertilisers & Chemicals Ltd.	5991577	3095139	-48.34
Himachal Futuristic Communications Ltd.	597917	1768561	195.79
Hindustan Lever Chemicals Ltd.	4089269	2935331	-28.22
Hindustan Motors Ltd.	13966580	2154671	-84.57
Hoechst Marion Roussel Ltd.	1404972	2423221	72.47
ICI India Ltd.	10426278	1298317	-87.55
Indian Oil Corporation Ltd.	1522542	2429451	59.56
Indian Shaving Products Ltd.	414486	619067	49.36
Ingersoll-Rand India Ltd.	1210517	571031	-52.83
Knoll Pharmaceuticals Ltd.	1142986	928247	-18.79
Madras Cements Ltd.	177060	225422	27.31
MRF Ltd.	899070	316384	-64.81
Nicholas Piramal India Ltd.	3390897	1196087	-64.73
Parke Davis (India) Ltd.	4366780	2519973	-42.29
Punjab Tractors Ltd.	1365111	3352752	145.6
SSI Ltd.	16176585	19080846	17.95
Supreme Industries Ltd.	3057148	1706159	-44.19
Thomas Cook (India) Ltd.	692291	683306	-1.298
Titan Industries Ltd.	13046228	2034913	-84.4

Torrent Pharmaceuticals Ltd.	3319146	224141	-93.25
Trent Ltd.	15322539	3576564	-76.66
Unichem Laboratories Ltd.	578635	143105	-75.27
United Phosphorus Ltd.	36495880	7742960	-78.78
Vatsa Corporation Ltd.	28732000	40886700	42.3
Videocon International Ltd.	85218002	32520846	-61.84
Voltas Ltd.	20618622	8206991	-60.2

Table 2 shows the growth in trading volumes in post-demat period when compared to pre-demat period. As is clear in the table, only 23% companies have shown positive growth in traded volumes and 77% of companies have shown negative growth in traded volumes. Again our hypothesis of no affect on traded volumes is accepted.

Possible Explanations

We have seen that demat has no favourable impact on liquidity as well as on returns to the investors. So our study is in direct contrast with the earlier study and also the theoretical arguments advanced for it. The possible reason can be that demat, when introduced first time in 1998 or 1999, stimulated investors' curiosity as well as the brokers, interest, hence it affected the liquidity as well as share prices in the stock exchanges positively. But later on when it became a general phenomenon, it did not carry any abnormal benefits to the investors. Once all the investors understand the merits and value of demat shares or when all shares are demated on all stock exchanges, the superior returns vanish.

V. CONCLUSION

This paper analysed the impact of compulsory dematerialization of BSE listed companies on the returns and liquidity of the companies. By applying the market adjusted model to estimate the normal returns, we have found that post-demat abnormal returns of the companies are not positive, rather they are negative. In case of traded volumes also, majority of the companies' experienced negative growth in traded volumes thereby rejecting the assumption of higher liquidity after demat. This may be so because demat has become a common phenomenon and stock exchanges have already discounted this information in the stock prices, so it does not carry any abnormal benefits for the investors.

References

Raju, M.T. and Patil, Prabhakar R., "Dematerialisation of Equity Shares in India: Liquidity, Returns and Volatility", www.utiicm.com/prabhakar_patil.html.

Bansal, Lalit K. (2001), "Merchant Banking and Financial Services," published by Unistar Books Pvt. Ltd., pp. 16.3-16.30.

Campbell, John Y, Andrew W. Lo, A Craig Mackinlay (1997), "The Econometrics of Financial Markets," Princeton University Press.

www.indiainfoline.com

Kullu Rao, P. (1996), "Custodial Services need for change," *Chartered Secretary*, October.

NSDL (1997), "A Handout," National Securities Depository Ltd., Bombay.

ANNEXURE

Name of company
Amara Raja Batteries Ltd.
Archies Greetings & Gifts Ltd.
Atlas Copco (India) Ltd.
Blue Star Ltd.
Carrier Aircon Ltd.
Electrosteel Castings Ltd.
Exide Industries Ltd.
German Remedies Ltd.
Gujarat Gas Company Ltd.
Gujarat State Fertilisers & Chemicals Ltd.
Himachal Futuristic Communications Ltd.
Hindustan Lever Chemicals Ltd.
Hindustan Motors Ltd.
Hoechst Marion Roussel Ltd.
ICI India Ltd.
Indian Oil Corporation Ltd.
Indian Shaving Products Ltd.
Ingersoll-Rand India Ltd.
Knoll Pharmaceuticals Ltd.
Madras Cements Ltd.
MRF Ltd.
Nicholas Piramal India Ltd.
Parke Davis (India) Ltd.
Punjab Tractors Ltd.
SSI Ltd.
Supreme Industries Ltd.
Thomas Cook (India) Ltd.
Titan Industries Ltd.
Torrent Pharmaceuticals Ltd.
Trent Ltd.
Unichem Laboratories Ltd.
United Phosphorus Ltd.
Vatsa Corporation Ltd.
Videocon International Ltd.
Voltas Ltd.

9

Corporate Reporting on the Internet by Leading Indian Companies

SUBHASH CHANDER AND MANJINDER SINGH

INTRODUCTION

Accounting information is irrefutable in a free enterprise economy. One cannot overemphasize the importance of availability of information to investors. Accounting information helps the present and potential investors in taking investment decisions. It assists the investors in selecting the best portfolio for their investments (Lal, Jawahar, 1985). The Trueblood Committee (1973) states that the basic objective of financial statements is to provide information useful for making economic decisions. Besides investors, information is significant from the point of view of large number of other potential users. Such potential users include, besides investors, lenders, suppliers, creditors, management, financial analysts, brokers and above all public at large. Empirical studies have shown that the information needs of the various users differ from each other (see Baker and Haslem, 1993; Buzby, 1974; Chandra Gyan, 1975;

Chenhall and Juchau, 1977; Banjamin and Stanga, 1977; and McNally, HockEng and Hasseldine, 1982). So in general accounting information is considered to be the chief means of reducing the uncertainty under which external users make decisions. Accounting information can be communicated to the users through various media; for example, prospectus, financial press releases, interim reports and paper-based annual reports. Within this portfolio of instruments, the paper-based corporate annual report is considered to be among the most important source of information in practice (see Arnold, Moizer and Noreen, 1984; Chang, Most and Brain, 1983; Pike, Meerjanssen and Chadwick, 1993 for importance of different information sources in the UK, US and Germany).

Although information given in paper-based annual reports is standardized and comparable etc. but due to the following limitations it is losing its relevance.

- There is a long time gap between the time when annual reports are prepared and got printed and the time they are received by users.
- Publication and distribution of printed corporate reports involves high printing, warehouses and delivery costs.
- Printed annual reports have limited circulations.
- Paper-based annual reports are unable to meet the needs of various user groups.
- It is very difficult to obtain paper-based financial statements for the past periods at the time of need.

In order to remove these limitations a new medium is emerging; i.e. Internet.

THE EMERGENCE OF INTERNET AND WEB REPORTING

Internet is one of the fastest developing communication channels today. It originated in 1960s as a communication tool for the American military establishment. It was deliberately constructed as a loose, multi-site medium of communication so that an enemy targeting a limited number of sites could not easily destroy it. Until the early 1990s, however, its use was limited to elite of specialists and there was no need to make it user friendly. Since 1991, the network has been a re-birth with the arrival of business users due to development of graphical user interface (world wide web). The world wide web (WWW) is a system within the internet which allows easy access by unsophisticated, non-specialist users being "hypertext" or linking system across the vast range of information provided on and accessed on the WWW by using a uniform resource locator (URL), an "address" which allows the web client to link up with the information required. The earliest commercial applications on the Internet were in the area of marketing and advertising and it continues to be the primary user in many businesses. However, it has recently extended into a support technology for other business users such as rates and other fulfilments.

Now-a-days corporations have started the use of Internet to inform the present and potential investors and also the other stakeholders with regard to company information. The companies are using their World Wide Web home page as a platform to present the financial data, especially annual reports, database on press releases and other company specific information. Studies conducted by researchers (Lymer, 1997; Deller, Stubnrath and Weber, 1997; Pirchegger, B., H. Schader and A. Wagenhofer, 1999; Marston and Leow, 1996) have proved that use of the web for financial reporting purpose has increased. WWW is now the single medium through which an organization communicates with audience; interactively is the unique feature of WWW, which has made it very popular.

PRIOR STUDIES AND DEVELOPMENTS IN CORPORATE REPORTING THROUGH THE INTERNET

Many organizations now report to their stakeholders via the Internet through their corporate websites. An important emphasis of this reporting activity has been on financial information. Securities market regulators and accounting professional bodies in some parts of the world have taken on a specific role to facilitate this practice. This includes the Securities and Exchange Commission (SEC) in the US through its Electronic Data Gathering and Retrieval System (EDGAR) and the Canadian securities administration through its Systems for Electronic Document Analysis and Retrieval (SEDAR) (Lymer *et al.*, 1999; Trites, 1999). The recent development of Extensible Business Reporting Language (XBRL) led by American Institute of Certified Practising Accountants (AICPA) could allow a consistent web-based environment for business reporting (Debreceny and Gray, 2001), propting an increase in the use if Internet for corporate reporting purposes.

The International Accounting Standards Committee (ISAC) recently commissioned a discussion paper for business reporting on the Internet (published as Lymer *et. al.*, 1999). The Canadian Institute of Accountants (CICA) (Trites, 1999) and the Financial Accounting Standards Board (FASB) in the US (FASB, 2000) have also taken initiatives in investigating electronics business reporting with emphasis on the Internet. Most recently the International Federation of Accountants (IFAC) has added to the professional pronouncements on this topic, developing the "code of conduct" for Internet-based reporting proposed in the IASC study (IFAC, 2002).

The IASC report (Lymer *et al.*, 1999) provided a survey of web-based financial reporting by the 30 largest corporation in 22 countries in Europe, Asia-Pacific, North and South America indicate that a large number of companies were undertaking web-based financial reporting but many of these were not fully utilizing the potential of the Internet. In an early study, Flynn and Gowthorpe (1977) while attempting to analyse the Internet reporting practice of 100 largest companies in the Fortune 500 list from a stakeholder perspective, state that the practice of Internet financial reporting is "sporadic and unsatisfactory."

Studies such as those by Ashbaugh *et. al.* (1999), FASB (2000) and Ettredge *et. al.* 2001 indicate that US corporations having been rapidly increasing the use of the Internet as corporate communication tool during the late 1990s. Moreover, Deller *et. al.* (1999) report that the US corporations use the Internet for investor relations more extensively than their counterparts in the UK and Germany.

Similar findings in relation to the increasing use of the Internet for financial reporting are reported by Lymer (1997) and Carven and Marston (1999) in the UK context (companies here seem to be the leaders in Internet reporting in Europe—see for instance Lymer *et. al.,* 1999), Lymer and Tallberg (1997) for corporations in Finland, Pirchegger and Wagenhofer (1999) for Australian companies, Rodrigues and Menezes (2001) for Portuguese companies, Marston and Wu (2001) for the Japanese case, Hassen *et. al.* (2000) on Malaysian companies, Oyelere *et. al.* (2000) for companies in New Zealand, Brennen & Hourigan (1998) for Irish companies, while Gowthrope and Amat (1999) discuss the infancy of the practices in Spain.

Several factors influencing levels and styles of reporting have been examined in the literature. These include company size, which appears to be positively associated with disclosure on the Internet*. Other factors may also be influential, such as spread of ownership (Oyelere *et. al.,* 2000). However, industrial grouping does not seem to be associated with reporting on the Internet (Craven and Marston, 1999, Lymer *et. al.* 1999, Rodrigues and Menezes, 2001) and neither does liquidity in at least the case of New Zealand (Oyelere *et. al.,* 2000).

RESEARCH OBJECTIVES

The paper has three specific objectives:

- Provide an overview of current Internet financial reporting in India. Emphasis is on what type of financial information is disclosed and how such information is presented on the Internet.
- Explain the reasons for *status quo* of Internet financial reporting in India.
- Formulate possible areas for future research on Internet corporate reporting in India.

---

* See Ashbaugh *et. al.* (1999), FASB (2000) and Ettredge *et. al.* (2001) for the US experience, Craven and Marston (1999) in the UK context, Pirchegger and Wagenhofer (1999) for Austrian companies, Rodrigues and Menezes (2001) for the Portuguese case and Marston and Wu (2001) for Japanese corporations.

RESEARCH METHODOLOGY AND DATA COLLECTION

The study is conducted to know the extent of web reporting practices in Indian Corporate sector. A sample of 15 leading companies from different sectors has been covered for this purpose. The list of sample companies has been shown in the Appendix I. Google search engine (http://www.google.com) was used to locate the home pages of each company. Private limited companies, Public limited companies and enterprises owned by the Government have been covered under the study.

The data collection started during January and lasted until the middle of February 2004. Websites differed in design and layout, so collecting data was not a routine process, and the speed of accessing the websites and downloading files varied among companies. The data collected relates to contents of information displayed by companies on their web sites. There are two approaches to collect the data one is direct access to websites and another is user's survey. Under present study 100% of data has been collected by approaching the websites of reporting companies via internet. The study investigated 23 attributes, for the most part, on the basis of existence/non-existence for each of the 15 websites. The full list of attributes used have been categorized into two main groups, general attributes and financial/annual report related attributes. General attributes focus on how financial information is presented on the internet with emphasis on whether the potential tools provided by the internet are used for disclosure. On the other hand, specific financial report attributes are related to the type of financial information that is presented on the internet. The full list of attributes used has been shown in Appendix II.

RESULTS

The analysis of the web sites of top 15 companies in India with regard to general attributes and financial report characteristics is provided in Tables 1 and 2. The evidence clearly suggests that most of the top 15 Indian companies are now placing same information on the Internet as they distribute through paper-based reports. Contact us and Search Boxes seem to dominate financial disclosure on the Internet. Site Maps, Downloads, Frequently Asked Questions, Disclaimers, and Press Releases are being used by just over half of the companies. Emphasis seems to be on directing users to search for a specific information rather than using technological tools offered by the Internet to enhance disclosure of financial information. Search Boxes provide benefits of ease of obtaining, and more timely information, the presentation of financial information is basically the same as that would be available in hardcopy form. Hence, full potential of the Internet is not used for corporate disclosure, suggesting a current lack of reliance on technology as a facilitator and motivator for change to traditional means of corporate reporting.

TABLE 1

General Attributes

Attributes	*Number*	*Percentage*
Site Map	12	80
Search Box	15	100
E-Mail alerts	4	27
Downloads	11	73
Contact Us	15	100
FAQ	8	53
Disclaimer	9	60
Press Releases	14	93

The financial report attributes build upon our results for general attributes providing further support to the fact that most Indian companies seem to be simply replicating paper-based report information on the Internet. The evidence clearly shows that all the 15 companies having their own web site, are providing financial information. The nature of financial information varies from company to company. Almost all the companies are concentrating on providing Balance Sheet, Income Statement, and Notes to financial statements, Financial Highlights, Interim Report. 14 companies are providing non-financial information. More than half of the sample companies are providing Director's Report, Segment Report, and Cash Flow Statement. Useful information such as share price performance is helpfully provided by 13 companies. About two-third of sample companies are providing Chairman's Message, Auditor's Report and Corporate Governance Report. A few of the companies are providing Financial Ratios and Significant Accounting Policies.

TABLE 2

Financial/Annual Report Related Attributes

Attributes	*Number*	*Percentage*
Director's Report	14	93
Chairman's Message	10	67
Financial Highlights	15	100
Balance Sheet	15	100
Income Statement	15	100
Cash Flow Statement	11	73
Auditor's Report	10	67
Financial Ratios	7	47
Management Analysis and Discussions	9	60
Interim Report	15	100
Non-Financial Information	14	93
Notes to Financial Statements	15	100
Segment Report	11	73
Significant Accounting Policies	5	33
Corporate Governance Report	10	67

DISCUSSIONS

A possible explanation for these findings could be the lack of initiatives on Internet financial reporting in India (see for instance, Ravlie, 2000, Khan, 2002). Regulatory pressure such as from the SEC (compulsory electronic listings on the EDGAR system) and Regulation Fair Disclosure in the US and SEDAR in Canada could have encouraged companies to increase their electronic reporting activity. Similarly, initiatives by accountancy institutes on electronic reporting such as the efforts of FASB and CICA, may also provide an impetus for electronic reporting in their respective countries. On-line financial reporting support and guidance has not been as dominant as in North America.

There is increasing academic research on Internet financial reporting in many countries to guide practice. This is glaringly absent in the India. Hence, research in this area is needed to guide practice and this paper attempts to be a starting point for this research.

In the absence of above mechanisms, Indian corporations could appear to be reluctant to disclose information on the Internet other than that required under statutory obligations for paper-based reports. The lack of reliability in Internet financial reporting is a key factor that could restrict the use of Internet for financial reporting in India. The lack of affordable broadband Internet access, IT skills shortage, and sustained privacy and security issue poses barriers to Indian businesses in participating in the information economy. These barriers are believed to undermine the gains from information technology for businesses and could explain the lower levels of Internet financial reporting than is the case elsewhere in the world.

LIMITATIONS OF THE STUDY

The present study gives an idea about the trend of web reporting practices in Indian corporate sector but the present work suffers from certain limitations which are as follows:

- The scope of the study is 15 companies. The sample of the study is limited. The results might have been different if we had adopted a big sample (50-100 companies)
- Under the present study only extent of web discloser by Indian companies have been analyzed. If a relationship between independent variables and extent of web discloser would have been analyzed, better results would have been obtained.
- Another limitation that this paper is subject to is that data collection from web sites depended upon the researcher's own browsing experience. Most

web sites were quite large and contained several sections, and some data may have been inadvertently missed.

SUMMARY, CONTRIBUTIONS AND IMPLICATIONS FOR FUTURE RESEARCH

This paper has highlighted that Internet financial reporting in India does not fully utilize the potential of the Internet to disclose corporate information. While factors such as lack of practical (regulatory) and academic initiatives. Bearing in mind its limitations this paper adds to the limited literature on Internet financial reporting in India. It provides an indication of the present practice and also outlines a useful research instrument that could be employed in other studies on corporate reporting on the Internet. The study also provides *prima facia* evidence that regulatory initiatives are needed in conjunction with academic research to provide an impetus to Indian corporations to fully utilize the potential of this phenomenal technology in providing corporate accountability to their various stakeholders.

Future research could expand the present study by investigating the Internet reporting practices of more corporations in India and comparing the results to the present study. Studies that compare the disclosure of financial information on the Internet in India with other countries would also be useful, with emphasis being on not just what is reported on the internet but also how it is reported.

Research into Internet reporting does not have to be merely restricted to financial reporting. Studies into disclosure of corporate governance coupled with social environmental information would be worthwhile research projects. These could focus on how such a practice can be facilitated and whether companies are actually using the WWW to disclose such information.

Internet corporate reporting research could also utilize traditional research methods such as surveys, interviews and case studies in conjunction with website analysis. This would enable a researcher to gather "richer data" and would also provide an indication of the context in which corporate reporting on the Internet takes place in organizations. These could be used for instance to investigate why Internet financial reporting in India does not fully utilize the potential benefits and tools provided by the Internet.

REFERENCES

Accounting Principles Board, Statement No. 4 (1970), "Basic Concept and Accounting Principles Underlying Financial Statements of Business Enterprises", New York, AICPA, p. 33.

American Accounting Association (1977), "Conceptual Framework for Financial Accounting and Reporting: Elements of Financial Statements and their Measurement", AAA, p. 19.

Angleys, F. (1978), "Meeting the Needs of the Users of Published Financial Statements", *The Chartered Accountant,* pp. 401-48.

Amold, John, Peter Moizer and Eric Noreen (1984), "Investment Appraisal Methods of Financial Analysts", (Spring): pp. 1-48.

Ashbaugh, H., K. Johnstne and T. Waterfield (1999), "Corporate Reporting on the Internet", *Accounting Horizons,* Vol. 13, No. 3, pp. 241-57.

Axelson and Kenneth, S. (1975), "A Businessman's View and Disclosure", *Journal of Accountancy,* p. 46.

Baker, H. Kent, Gaslem and John, A. (1973), "Information Needs of Individual Investors", *The Journal of Accountancy,* (November): pp. 64-69.

Batra, G.S. and Garner, P. (1998), *Accounting Theory and Practice,* Deep and Deep Publications, New Delhim pp. 235-43.

Beaver, William, H. (1978), "Current Trends in Corporate Disclosure", *The Journal of Accountancy,* pp. 44-52.

Benjamin, James, J. and Stanga, Keith, G. (1977), "Difference in Disclosure Needs of Major Users of Financial Statements", *Accounting and Business Research,* (Summer): pp. 187-99.

Bell, B.A. (1998), "Corporate Web Sites and Securities Offerings", *New York Law Journal,* Vol. 219, No. 97, pp. 5-7.

Bencivenga, D. (1998), "Investors Push for Real Time Data on Internet", *New York Law Journal,* Vol. 219, No. 87, pp. 5-7.

Birnberg, Jacob, G. and Dopuch, Nicholas (1963), "A Conceptual Approach to the Framework for Disclosure", *The Journal of Accountancy,* pp. 56-62.

Buzby, Stephen (1974), "Selected Items of Information and their Disclosure in Annual Reports, *The Accounting Review,* (July): pp. 423-33.

Buzby, Stephen (1974), "The Nature of Adequate Disclosure", *The Journal of Accountancy,* p. 37.

C. Gowthorpe and G. Flynn (1997), "Reporting on the web: The State of the Art", *Accountancy,* (August): pp. 68-69.

Cairncross, Frances (1997), "A Survey of Telecommunications: A Connected World", *The Economy,* September 13th, pp. 1-42.

Chander, Subhash (1992), *Corporate Reporting Practices,* New Delhi, Deep and Deep Publications.

Chandra, Gyan (1974), "A Study of the Consensus on Disclosure Among Public Accountants and Security Analysts", *The Accounting Review,*

(October): pp. 733-42.

Chandra, Gyan (1975), "Information Needs of Security Analysis", *The Journal of Accountancy*, (December): pp. 65-70.

Chang, Lucia, S. Kenneth, S. Most and Carlos, W. Brain (1983), "The Utility of Annual Reports: An International Study", *Journal of International Business Studies*, (Spring/Summer), pp. 63-83.

Chenhall, R.H. and Juchau, R. (1977), "Investor Information Needs—An Australian Study", *Accounting and Business Research*, (Spring): pp. 111-19.

Cook, Michael J. and H. Sutton (1995), "Summary Annual Reporting: A Cure for Information Overload", *Financial Executive*, (January/February): pp. 12-15.

Cooper, W.W., Ijiri, Yuji (1984), "Kohler's Dictionary for Accountants, Prentice Hall of India, Pvt. Ltd., New Delhi.

Deller, D.M. Stubenrath and C. Weber (1999), "A Survey of the Use of the Internet for Investor Relations in the USA, UK and Germany", *European Accounting Review*, Vol. 8, No. 2.

Duff and Phelops (1976), "*A Management Guide to Better Financial Reporting*, Arthur Anderson and Co.

Elgin, Peggie, R. (1996), "IR Pros-tab Internet to Reach Investor", Track Rumors", *Corporate Cash-Flow*, (January): pp. 3-4.

Elliott, Robert, K.C. (1997), "The Third Wave Breaks on the Shores of Accounting", *Accounting Horizons*, Vol. 6, No. 2, pp. 61-85.

Ellis, Charles, D. (1985), "How to Manage Investor Relations", *Financial Analysts Journal*, (March/April): pp. 34-41.

Ettredge, M., V.J. Richardson, and S. Scholz (1998a), "The Presentation of Financial Information at Corporation Web Sites" Working Paper, University of Kansas.

Ettredge, M., V.J. Richardson, and S. Scholz (1998b), "Financial Data at Corporate Web Sites: Do Information Clientless matter?" Working Paper, University of Kansas.

Ettredge, M., V.J. Richardson, and S. Scholz (1999a), "Determinants of Voluntary Dissemination of Financial Data at Corporate Web Sites.", Working Papers, University of Kansas.

Ettredge, M., V.J. Richardson, and S. Scholz (1999b), "Financial Data at Corporate Web Sites: Does User Sophistication Matter?" *Working Paper*, University of Kansas.

Ettredge, M., V.J. Richardson, and S. Scholz (1999c), "Going Concern Auditor Reports at Corporate Web Sites: A Regulatory Loophole?" *Working Paper*, University of Kansas.

Ettredge, M., V.J. Richardson, and S. Scholz (1999d), "Accounting Information at Corporate Web Sites: Does the Auditor's Opinion Matter?" *Working Paper*, University of Kansas.

Farell, Joseph and Garth, Saloner (1985), "Installed Base and Compatibility-Innovation, Product Preannouncements and Predation", *American Economic Review*, Vol. 76, No. 5, pp. 940-55.

Financial Accounting Standard Board, Business Reporting Research Project, "Electronic Distribution of Business Reporting Information", FASB.

Financial Accounting Standard Board, Statement of Financial Accounting Concept No. 1 (1979), "Objectives of Financial Reporting by Business

Enterprises", *Journal of Accountancy*, (February), pp. 90-98.

Fulkerson, Jennifer (1996), "How Investor use Annual Reports", *American Demographics*, (May), p. 16.

G. Green and B. Spaul (1997), "Digital Accountability", *Accountancy*, (May), pp. 64-65.

G.L. Helms and J. Mancino (1998), "The Electronic Auditors", *Journal of Accountancy*, (April), pp. 45-48.

Gowthorpe, C. and G. Flynn (1997), "Reporting on the web: The State of the Art", *Accounting*, Vol. 120, No. 1248, pp. 58-59.

Gowthorpe, C. and O. Amat (1999), "External Reporting of Accounting and Financial Information via the Internet in Spain", *European Accounting Review*, p. 12.

Grover, Ray J. (1994), "Financial Disclosure: When More is nor Better", *Financial Executive*, (May/June), pp. 11-14.

Haggie, David (1984), "The Annual Report as an Aid to Communication", *Accountancy*, (August), pp. 66-67.

Hay, Report, D. (1955), "Management Thinking Concerning Annual Reports", *The Accounting Review*, (July), pp. 440-50.

Heldin, P. (1999), "The Internet as a Vehicle for Investors Information: The Swedish Case", *European Accounting Review*, p. 12.

J. Sulph (1998), "A Question of Trust", *Accounting*, (March), pp. 45-48.

Jenkins and Edmund, L. (1994), "An Information Highway in Need of Capital Improvement", *Journal of Accountancy*, (May), pp. 77-78.

Katz, Michael, L. and Carl Shapiro (1985), "Network Externalities, Competition and Compatibility", *American Accounting Review*, Vol. 75, No. 3, pp. 424-40.

Koreto, R.J. (1997), "When the Bottom Line is Online", *Journal of Accountancy*, Vol. 183, No. 3, pp. 63-65.

Lal, Jawahar (1985), *Corporate Annual Reports: Theory and Practice*, New Delhi, Sterling Publishers Private Limited.

Lal, Jawahar (1988), *Contemporary Accounting Issues*, New Delhi: Vision Books.

Lee, T.A. (1976), *Financial Reporting-Issues and Analysis*, Thomas Nelson and Sons.

Louwers, T.J., W.R. Pasewark and E.W. Typpo (1996), "The Internet: Changing the Way Corporation Tell their Story", *CPA Journal*, Vol. 66, No. 11, pp. 24-28.

Lowerngard, Mary (1997), "The Internet as Mass Leader", *Institutional Investors*, (April), pp. 104-06.

Lymer, Andrew (1997), "The use of the Internet for Corporate Reporting—A discussion of the issues and survey usage in the U.K.", *Journal of Financial Information System, Working Papers*, Birmingham.

Mc Cafferty, J. (1995), "How Much to Reveal Online", *CFO: The Magazine for Senior Financial Executives*, pp. 11-12.

NcNally, G.M., HockEng, Lee, Hasseldine and C. Roy (1982), "Corporate Financial Reporting in New Zealand: An analysis of Users Preferences and Disclosure Practices for Discretionally Information", *Accounting and Business Research*, (Winter), pp. 11-20.

Miller, R. and M.R. Young (1997), "Financial Reporting and Risk Management in the 21st Century", *Fordham Law Review*, Vol. 65, No. 5, pp. 1987-2064.

Mahoney, William, F. and Charles, K. Wessendorf (1996), "How to Get Investors Online", *Financial Executive,* (January/February), pp. 41-43.

National Investor Relations Institute (1996), "Investor Relations Surveys: Utilizing Technology in the Practice of Investors' Relations, Washington: NIRI.

Parker, L.D. (1982), "Corporate Annual Reporting Perspective", *Accounting and Business Research,* (Autumn), pp. 279-86.

Petravick, S. and J.W. Gillett (1996), "Financial Reporting on the World Wide Web", *Management Accounting* (USA), Vol. 78, No. 5, pp. 26-29.

Petravick, S. and J.W. Gillett (1998), "Distributing Earning Reports on the Internet", *Management Accounting* (USA), Vol. 8, No. 4, pp. 54-64.

Pike, Richard, Johannes Meerjanssen and Leslie Chadwick (1993), "The Appraisal of Ordinary Shares by Investment Analysis in the UK and Germany", *Accounting and Business Research,* Vol. 23, No. 92, pp. 489-99.

Pirchegger, B., H. Schader and A. Wagenhofer (1999), "Financial Information on the Internet – A Survey of the Homepage of Austrian Companies", *European Accounting Review,* p. 12.

Prentice, R., V.J. Richardson and S. Scholz (1999a), "Corporate Web Sites Disclosure and Rule 10b-5—An Empirical Evaluation", *American Business Law Journal,* Vol. 36, No. 4, pp. 531-78.

Prentice, R., V.J. Richardson and S. Scholz (1999b), "Caught in the web", *Financial Executive,* (September/October), pp. 27-28.

Prentice, R.A. (1998), "The Future of Corporate Disclosure: The Internet, Securities Fraud, and Rule 10b-5", *Emory Law Journal,* Vol. 47, No. 1, pp. 1-88.

Smith, James, E. and Smith, Nara, P. (1971), "Readability: A Major Communication Function of Financial Reporting", *The Accounting Review,* (July), pp. 552-61.

Sorter, H.G. (1996), "An Event Based Approach to Basic Accounting Theory", *Accounting Review,* (January), pp. 12-19.

Stevens, M.G. (1999), "Financial Information is Flooding the Internet", *The Practical Accountant,* (February), p. 24.

Trites, G.D. (1999), "The Impact Technology of Financial and Business Reporting", CICA Research Study (Draft).

Wager, L.K. (1998), "Safe Harbors in Cyberspace", *New York Law Journal,* Vol. 220, No. 36, pp. 3-28.

Wallmann and Steven, M.H. (1995), "The Future of Accounting and Disclosure in an Evolving World: The Need for Dramatic Change", *Accounting Horizons,* Vol. 9, No. 3, pp. 81-91.

Waroff, Deborah (1995), "IR On-line", *Institutional Investors,* Vol. 29, No. 4, p. 37.

APPENDIX I

List of Companies Included in the Survey and their Sectors

Sr. No.	Name of the Company	Market Cap. (Rs. bn)	Web Address	Sector
1.	Oil & Natural Gas Corporation Ltd.	1050.91	www.ongcindia.com	
2.	Hindustan Lever Ltd.	435.08	www.hll.com	
3.	Indian Oil Corporation Ltd.	380.93	www.indiaoil.com	
4.	Wipro Ltd.	367.31	www.wipro.com	
5.	Infosys Technology	354.36	www.info.com	
6.	State Bank of India	325.15	www.sbi.com	
7.	ITC Ltd.	250.17		
8.	ICICI Bank Ltd.	195.30	www.icici.com	
9.	Gas Authority of India Ltd.	190.82		
10.	Steel Authority of India Ltd.	182.15		
11.	Ranbaxy Laboratories Ltd.	182.09	www.ranbaxy.com	
12.	Tata Engineering & Locomotive Co. Ltd.	173.23	ww.tatamotors.com	
13.	Hindustan Petroleum Corporation Ltd.	162.06		
14.	TISCO	157.06	www.tatasteel.com	
15.	Bharat Heavy Electricals Ltd.	149.17	www.bhel.com	

Appendix II

General and Financial/Annual Report Related Attributes

Attributes

General Attributes

1. Site Map
2. Search Box
3. E-Mail alerts
4. Downloads
5. Contact Us
6. FAQ
7. Disclaimer
8. Press Releases

Financial/Annual Report Related

9. Director's Report
10. Chairman's Message
11. Financial Highlights
12. Balance Sheet
13. Income Statement
14. Cash Flow Statement
15. Auditor's Report
16. Financial Ratios
17. Management Analysis and Discussions
18. Interim Report
19. Non-Financial Information
20. Notes to Financial Statements
21. Segment Report
22. Significant Accounting Policies
23. Corporate Governance Report

10

Strength of Moving Average as a Technical Indicator

A Study of Indian Capital Markets

MOHIT GUPTA, NAVDEEP AGGARWAL AND S.K. SINGLA

Weak form of market efficiency, worldwide, invites application of technical analysis for profitable investment strategies. Indian reportedly is a weak-efficient market and therefore is no different a case. We applied the technique of moving averages to check the profitability of technical analysis in India. The results are very encouraging, and stand much higher than the returns offered by other investment avenues like fixed deposits in banks and debt-based mutual funds. Further the technique being mechanical in nature does not need any specific fundamental knowledge and therefore offers an easy investment tool for small investors.

There has been a major economic transition in Indian economy in the last decade. An integral part of the economic reform process has been the financial sector reforms, which involve reshaping of the market structure, innovations in the financial instruments and practices and a more comprehensive regulatory environment.

Researchers have argued that when economies pass through transition period, experience a rapid flow of quantum information in their capital markets. The reform process at the same time is expected to enhance the organisational efficiency of the stock market system whereby ensuring that the evolved market structure exhibits a better capacity to absorb additional economic and other relevant information. However, if quantum of information is too large for the stock market system to reflect it fully and instantaneously, the capital market will plunge to state of market inefficiency. This implies that technical analysis or the study of the past share price reliably forecast future share prices and lead investors to return which exceeds the market. For example, study using moving averages was conducted on Dow Jones Industrial index, taking in to account 25,000 trading days in which it was found that stock markets are inefficient and above normal returns can be made using technical indicators (Brock *et. al.*, 1992). Moreover, fundamental analysis, because of enormous amount of information necessary and enormous amount of time required to obtain all the fundamental factors is usually too costly and time consuming for the small investors. In addition, the institutional investors and the corporate insiders are armed with secret information not available to small investors. But the input requirement of technical analysis mainly stock price and volume is easily available to all. Technical analysis is probably the only forecasting technique an individual investor can utilize.

The technical analysis system of security evaluation has been extensively tested for many developed (for example, Ball and Officer, 1989) and developing capital markets (for instance, Dawson, 1985). Especially in 1990s, with the easier accessibility to financial data banks and greater computer power, a thorough demonstration of the benefits of technical trading rules and consequently the possibility of forecasting financial asset returns were studied by many researchers. Certain techniques like moving average have shown power to detect non-linearity and have predictive power (Neftci, 1991).

Recent studies on the Indian capital market support the argument by concluding that the Indian market is weak form efficient (e.g., Gupta, 1997). In the Indian context also some studies and surveys have been done by brokers and in-house researchers, which are mainly supplied to elite clients and not published as piece of research. Despite the existence of organized capital markets for a long time, there has been hardly any systematic evaluation of technical school of thought and development of investment strategy solely on the basis of technical analysis. The present study has been conducted to plug this gap.

DATA AND METHODOLOGY

The data for the present study consisted of daily prices of NSE (National Stock Exchange) Nifty-50 index from 1.1.96 to 30.9.03 (www.nseindia.com). This actually resulted in data of 1936 trading days. The moving average technique is applied on closing price of Index.

We have used the index in place of any security as in present era it is possible to buy and short sell index futures. Index usually has less volatility as compared to individual stock and the diversification benefit by holding the index as security is inherently there. Moreover, the margin requirement on index is generally less as compared to stocks, thereby resulting in better yield.

For the purpose of analysis, two approaches have been used: 'Buy-square off' and 'Always in the market' . In "Buy-square off' approach, a buy signal is generated when the ratio of closing price to the particular moving average is greater than 1; the buy action is then performed on the opening price of next trading day. The position is held till the sell signal is generated, that is when the ratio of closing price of index to a particular moving average is less than 1. As soon as the sell signal appears, the sell action is performed at the opening price of the next trading day. This approach involves the holding of index as security for the time period when only buy signal is in force; the position is nil in time period of sell signal. This is a mechanical system and requires the ratios to be generated and actions taken accordingly.

Under the "Always in the market" approach, the buy signal is generated when the ratio of closing price to the particular moving average is greater than 1; buy action is performed at the opening price of the next trading day. This holding is squared off when the sell signal is generated, that is when the ratio of closing price of index to a particular moving average is less then 1; sell action is performed at the opening price of next trading day. In this approach whenever the sell (or buy) signal is generated and the previous holding is squared off, the opposite trade is entered into. This implies that whenever sell signal is generated to square off previously held long position (say 1 lot), instead of selling one lot, two lots are sold, one for the squaring off previous long position, and other is entered as a fresh short position. This further implies that when sell position is to be squared off (buy signal is generated), instead of buying 1 lot, again 2 lots are bought, one for squaring of previous short position and other is fresh entry as long position. By this approach we are always in the market, maintaining one of either position – long or short.

We have not compared the results of the two approaches as this would be akin to comparing apples and oranges. Nor we have demonstrated the comparison of returns from the investment in index on the basis of fundamental analysis and technical analysis (using moving average as technical indicator). We have just concentrated on the argument that a continuous investment strategy can be designed by use of moving average based system in Indian capital markets. Comparison of the two approaches (fundamental or technical) to investment is not appreciated because of different bases used for the two. But the point of concern is that the use of mechanical based trading system provides the ease and mechanical steps that counteract even the behavioural inefficiencies on the part of humans, while investing.

Under both the approaches, technical indicators used are 21 day moving average (DMA), 50 DMA, 100 DMA and 200 DMA. The study does not take into account the percentage return earned keeping in view that in futures market, leverage effect is at the play. Since in both the approaches the investment in index futures is in the form of initial and mark to market margin, the exercise of calculating the returns is complex and futile as there is constant cash flow in the mark to market margin account, which may give exorbitant annualized returns/losses.

Various descriptive parameters have been calculated, namely, range of profits, range of losses, average profit, average loss, number of profitable trades, number of loss trades, total profit, total loss, absolute cash flow and average profit/loss per trade. For simplification we have not taken into account the spreads between future prices of subsequent months.

RESULTS

Buy-square off Approach

The various descriptive parameters under this approach are given in Table 1. The maximum profit earned in case of 21 DMA, 50 DMA, 100 DMA and 200 DMA came out to be Rs. 36340, 83660, 79200 and 92330 respectively. The minimum profit was Rs. 140, 2500, 590 and 610 respectively. Similarly, the maximum loss incurred using different DMA's was Rs. 20840, 20840, 15250, 22790 respectively in case of 21 DMA, 50DMA, 100DMA and 200DMA. The minimum loss was Rs. 80, 80, 180 and 780 respectively. The net cash flows in case of 21 DMA, 50 DMA, 100 DMA and 200 DMA stood at Rs. 247240, 162120, 184930 and 15100 respectively.

The percentage return figures were 549%, 360%, 411% and 50% respectively in case of 21 DMA, 50 DMA, 100 DMA and 200 DMA. Out of these figures returns using 200 DMA, seems to be odd man out. The reason behind this is very slow responsiveness of 200 DMA to market prices. Still, the use of moving average is a profitable investment tool in Indian stock markets.

Always in the Market Approach

The various descriptive parameters under this approach are given in Table 2. The results were far more encouraging in this case. The maximum profit earned in case of 21 DMA, 50 DMA, 100 DMA and 200 DMA came out to be Rs. 45600, 83660, 79200 and 92330 respectively. The minimum profit was Rs. 120, 1800, 480 and 420 respectively. Similarly, the maximum loss incurred using different DMA's was Rs. 20840, 20840, 15250, 25810 respectively in case of 21 DMA, 50 DMA,

TABLE I

Buy-Square Approach

Parameter	*21 DMA*	*50 DMA*	*100 DMA*	*200 DMA*
Profit (Max.)	36340	83660	79200	92330
(Min.)	140	2500	590	610
Loss (Max.)	20840	20840	15250	22790
(Min.)	80	80	180	780
Nifty Points Covered for Max. Profit	182	418	396	462
Nifty Points Covered for Max. Loss	104	104	76	114
Max. Profit/Max. loss	1.74	4.01	5.19	4.05
Min. Profit/Min. loss	1.75	31.25	3.28	0.78
No. of Profit trades	32	12	10	4
No. of Loss trades	51	27	14	27
Total Profit	458060	305880	254250	178920
Total Loss	190900	134400	63560	156380
Transaction cost	19920	9360	5760	7440
Net Cash flow	247240	162120	184930	15100
Total trades	83	39	24	31
Per cent profit trades	39	31	42	13
Average Profit per profit trade	14314	25490	25425	44730
Average Loss per loss trade	3743	4978	4540	5792
Per Cent Return on Rs. 45000*	**549**	**360**	**411**	**50**

* Rs. 45000 is the initial margin considering 15% initial margin on average Nifty level of 1500 and one lot of Nifty future consists of 200 units.

100 DMA and 200 DMA. The minimum loss was Rs. 80, 80, 180 and 460 respectively. The net cash flows in case of 21 DMA, 50 DMA, 100 DMA and 200 DMA stood at Rs. 387000, 257400, 300294 and (-40170) respectively.

The percentage return figures were 860%, 572%, 667% and (-90%) respectively in case of 21 DMA, 50 DMA, 100 DMA and 200 DMA. Again the returns using 200 DMA, are undesirable. The reason behind this is again attributable to the slow responsiveness of 200 DMA to market prices.

CONCLUSION

Weak form of market efficiency, worldwide, invites application of technical analysis for profitable investment strategies. Indian reportedly is a weak-efficient market and

TABLE 2

Always in the Market Approach

Parameter	*21 DMA*	*50 DMA*	*100 DMA*	*200 DMA*
Profit (Max.)	45600	83660	79200	92330
(Min.)	120	1800	480	420
Loss (Max.)	20840	20840	15250	25810
(Min.)	80	80	180	460
Nifty Points Covered for Max. Profit	228	418	396	462
Nifty Points Covered for Max. Loss	104	104	76	129
Max. Profit / Max. loss	2.19	4.01	5.19	3.58
Min. Profit / Min. loss	1.50	22.50	2.67	0.91
No. of Profit trades	64	27	20	9
No. of Loss trades	101	53	28	52
Total Profit	857420	570140	432264	273950
Total Loss	430820	293540	120450	299480
Transaction cost	39600	19200	11520	14640
Net Cash flow	387000	257400	300294	-40170
Total trades	165	80	48	61
Per cent profit trades	39	34	42	15
Average Profit per profit trade	13397	21116	21613	30439
Average Loss per loss trade	4266	5539	4302	5759
Per Cent Return on Rs. 45000*	**860**	**572**	**667**	**-90**

* Rs. 45000 is the initial margin considering 15% initial margin on average Nifty level of 1500 and one lot of Nifty future consists of 200 units.

therefore is no different a case. We applied the technique of moving averages using 4 type of moving averages, namely, 21 DMA, 50 DMA, 100 DMA and 200 DMA, to check the profitability of technical analysis in India. It was only in the case of 200 DMA that the results were not appreciable. This can be attributed to its slow responsiveness as the length of 200 DMA is very large and number of profitable trades gets drastically reduced. Still the results are very encouraging, and stand much higher than the returns offered by other investment avenues like fixed deposits in banks and debt-based mutual funds. Further the technique being mechanical in nature does not need any specific fundamental knowledge and therefore offers an easy investment tool for small investors.

REFERENCES

Ball, R. and R.R. Officer (1989), "Try This is Your Chartist," in Ball, R. ed. *Share Price and Portfolio Theory*.

Brock, W., J. Lakonishok and B. Lebaron (1992), "Technical Trading Rules and the Stockastic Properties of Stock Returns," *Journal of Finance*, Vol. 47: 1731-64.

Dawson, S.M. (1985), "Share Recommendations Using Technical Analysis," *Asia-Pacific Journal of Management*: 180-88.

Gupta, O.P. (1997), "A Re-examination of Weak Form Efficiency of Indian Stock Market," *Finance India*, September.

Neftci, S.N. (1991), "Naïve Trading Rules in Financial Markets and Weiner-Kolmogorov Prediction Theory: A Study of Technical Analysis," *Journal of Business*, Vol. 64: 549-71.

11

Mutual Funds Industry in India

Resurgence and Prospects

JASPAL SINGH AND POONAM SHARMA

The period from 1993 to 2001 has seen both slump and boom in Indian capital market. A rising trend has been noticed in case of domestic savings in India. A mixed positive trend in case of foreign investments coming to India along with unstable corporate profits has also been noticed. Global events do cast their shadow on capital markets in India also. The stock indices dance to the tune of NASDAQ movement in USA. International events like terrorists attack in New York or outbreak of war in Afghanistan or Iraq do dampen the spirit of Indian investors. Media sensitive Indian investor will create selling pressure in stock markets even on petroleum Minister's expression in media to increase diesel prices without waiting to see when the proposal gets mature. Tech savvy Indian stock markets immediately reflect any bad news, thus, further weakening the overall market sentiments. As a mutual fund invests its pooled money in capital markets which in turn depends upon economic growth of a country, thus, in this turbulent environment, the question to be answered is: What prospects do mutual fund industry has in India? In this paper, looking at the current economic scenario, an attempt has been made to assess the future prospects of mutual funds in India.

Mutual funds put the pooled money of small investors in company's stocks, government securities, bonds, etc. Any downtrend in stock prices would have ripple effect on earnings of mutual funds' investment. Similarly, any rates cut announced by the government on securities or bank deposits etc. will also do the same. Hence, the aspects of:

1. Country's economic health and its future,
2. Government regulation of funds, and
3. Effective management by professional fund managers,

have an important role to play in deciding the fate of mutual fund industry in India.

OVERVIEW OF ECONOMIC GROWTH IN INDIA

First of all, let us take a look at the economic growth in India, since independence in general and particularly in the last decade. (see Fig. 1)

FIG. 1

The Indian Economy: 1950-2001

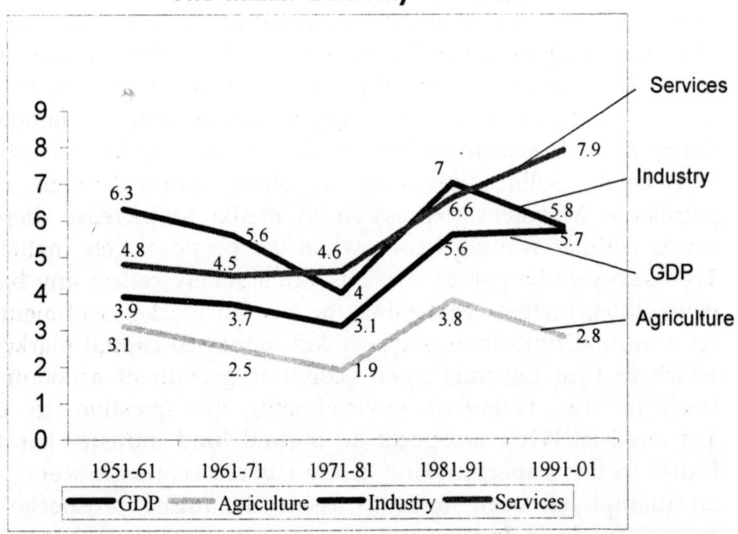

Source: RBI, Planning Commission, CMIEBT., *Business Today*, Jan. 2002.

Starting from GDP rate of 3.9% in 1951-52, it has been hovering around 6.0% in the last decade from 1991-92 to 2000-01. The persistent political problem in middle-east and the outbreak of war between US and Iraq during mid-2003 lead to the rise in oil prices. Despite these constraints, growth in real GDP in 2004-05 as given in Interim Budget is expected to be 7.5 to 8 per cent. This growth rate marks the revitalizing Indian Economy. Agriculture sector growth has been moving in the range of 3.1% in 1951-61 to 2.8% in 1991-2001. However, the good monsoon during 2003 has fuelled the growth of the economy. On the other hand, industrial growth has been quiet erratic and in the decade 1991-2001 it has shown deceleration and has come down to 5.8% as against 7.0% in 1981-91. In the year 2001-02 it has been reported at 2.8%. This is because of decrease in demand and other factors. As per the economic development history the world over, economies move from being agriculture-lead to industry-lead to being services-lead. But India has transited from agriculture to services. Therefore, it is only services sector that has posted handsome growth since 1971-72 and has touched 7.9% in the last decade. Also, inflation rate according to Wholesale Price Index (WPI) declined to 1.87% for the month ending June, 2002 from 7.0% at the year start.

The per capita income has been on the rise since 1950-51 and more sharply over the last decade. Food production has also posted consistent gains. Gross domestic capital formation has been rising but slowly and after a spurt in its growth in 1990-91 has decelerated in the year 2000-01. However, after opening up of the economy to private sector in 1991 it has risen sharply. In Gross domestic savings category, household sector has recorded consistent growth, which has been moving in consonance with the growth in mutual fund industry. Forex reserves have grown to a whooping level (touching $100 billion mark by the end of Dec., 2003) that hints at the growing strength of the Indian economy. But noticeable point is growth in government expenditure that has doubled in the last decade. Portfolio investment after making its opening in Sept., 1992 with meager amount of $4 million has touched the level of $3026 millions in the year 2000-01. The trend shows that growing economies have always been lucrative for investors the world over.

GROWTH IN THE INDIAN MUTUAL FUND INDUSTRY

The growth potential, which the economy has, cannot be denied. Cyclic movements in the economic growth cycle, however, could not be ruled out. Mutual fund industry, as it is a part and parcel of the economy will be moving with the movement in the Indian economy. Fig 2 depicts that how over the years mutual funds industry in India grew and the assets being managed by it. This clearly brings out the importance of this investment channel in the Indian economy. Noticeably, at times when share index had not been doing well, even then, mutual funds maintained their overall position in the Indian capital market. Fig. 2 shows that in the year 1992-93 the assets under fund management were Rs. 46988.02 crores. But after the private sector mutual funds were allowed to enter the Indian market assets under fund management grew to Rs. 61301.21 crores in 1993-94 and touched the figure of Rs. 107946.10 crores in 1999-00. After falling back to Rs. 90587 crores in 2000-01 it has again risen to Rs. 94571.0 crores in the year 2001. Despite the sensex fall in 2001-02, mutual funds industry withered the onslaught and managed to maintain assets under their management to Rs. 101821.80 crores which ultimately settled at Rs. 109299.8 crores by the end of March, 2003.

Table 1 depicts that the mutual funds are the first choice of individual investors in all the mutual fund sectors, i.e. Private, Public and UTI.

The Table 1 shows the investors pattern in mutual fund industry. In all the sectors, i.e. private, public and UTI the majority investors are individuals and small investors as against corporate bodies, both Indian and overseas and Institutional Investors. On overall basis, the individual investors (2.44) crores are the maximum as compare to other categories. This points out to the fact that small investors still prefer to depend upon the expertise of mutual fund professional managers for looking after their capital market investments.

FIG. 2

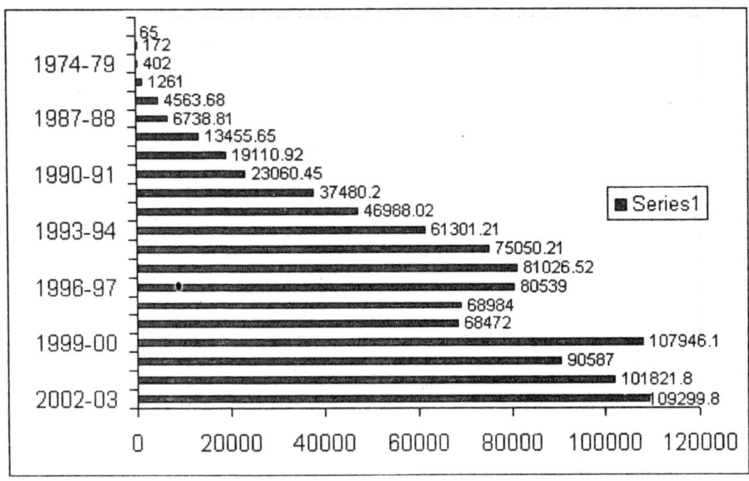

Source: SEBI and AMFI as quoted in *Business Times*, Jan. 2002, p. 69 and modified.

TABLE I

Mutual Funds Investors Pattern

(In percentages)

	Individuals	*Corporate and Institutions*	*NRIs, OCBs and FIIs*	*Total*
Private Sector	96.70	0.89	3.11	100
Public Sector	97.95	0.41	1.64	100
UTI	98.37	0.47	1.16	100
Overall Average	98.04	1.46	0.50	100
Investors (crores)	(2.44)	(0.41)	(0.23)	(3.08)

Source: SEBI as quoted in *Financial Express*, p. 1, August 13, 2002.

FUTURE PROSPECTS OF INDIAN ECONOMY

As regards prospects, inflation around 4 to 4.5%, estimates for GDP growth has been set around 7.5 to 8% during 2004-05. Forex reserves have already touched the figure of $100 billion by Dec., 2003. The estimates, however, paint a reasonably bright future for the Indian capital markets to move in a positive direction.

Following are the major highlights of the Monthly Economic Report (Jan. 2004) issued by the Ministry of Finance, Department of Economic Affairs:

1. The winter season rainfall up to Jan. 28, 2004 was normal/excess in 53% of meteorological sub-divisions.
2. Food grains stocks was 24.41 million tons as on Jan. 1, 2004.
3. Overall industrial growth was 6.2% in April-Nov. 2003-04 as compared with 5.4% in April-Nov. 2002-03.
4. Core infrastructure sectors achieved an average growth rate of 4.2% in April-Nov. 2003-04 as compared with 6.1%in April-Nov. 2002-03.
5. Broad money (M3) growth was 11.3% during the period March 31, 2003 to Jan. 9, 2004. Annual growth as on Jan. 9, 2004 was 13.5%.
6. The annual inflation rate in terms of WPI (base 1993-94) was 6.13% for week ended Jan. 17, 2004 as compared with 4.42% a year ago.
7. Exports and Imports increased by 13.5% and 24.9% in April-Dec. 2003-04 as compared with 18% and 15% in 2002-03.
8. Rupee depreciated against US dollar, Pound sterling, Euro and Japanese Yen in Dec. 2003.
9. Forex reserves (excluding gold and SDR'S) stood at $97.62 billion at the end of Dec. 2003.
10. Tax revenue (net to centre) during April-Dec. 2003-04 higher by 14.4% over April, Dec. 2002-03
11. Fiscal deficit during April-Dec. 2003-04 is 60.2% of the budget estimates as compared with 63.7% in the corresponding period of the last year.

Regarding the aspect of government's role for economic growth prospects in India, the initiatives taken by it to pull out the economy from recessionary pressures are applaudable. Some of the facts (see Sebi.com fact sheet) as regards current situation in relation to the governance of securities market in India are:

1. Two national level exchanges (Bombay Stock Exchange—BSE and National Stock Exchange—NSE) and 21 regional exchanges with fully electronic trading platforms and around 9400 broking outfits, of which 29 are foreign brokers.
2. 9600 companies listed on exchanges with market capitalization hovering around US $ 125.5 billion.
3. The turnover of NSE and BSE, in financial year 2001-02, was around US $ 102 Billion and US $ 62 Billion respectively.
4. Total of 99.9% of the trades are settled in dematerialized form in a T+3 rolling settlement environments.
5. Negligible trade failure of .003% of the total traded value in financial year 2001-02.
6. Trades are guaranteed by clearing corporation/ house of the exchanges. Further, the exchanges have Settlement Guarantee Funds to meet with any unpredictable situation.
7. Exchanges run by non-member directors as a prelude to corporatisation and demutualization.
8. Two central depositories National Securities Depository Ltd. (NSDL) and Central Depository Services Ltd. (CDSL) with nation-wide presence through their 380 members. More than 90% of the Market capitalization is in the electronic form.
9. Efficiency in the system has resulted into the transaction cost in Indian Securities Market being one of the lowest in the world.
10. 38 Mutual Funds with 396 schemes having an asset base of nearly US $ 21.96 Billion.
11. Presence of 498 Foreign Institutional Investors (FIIs) and their 1325 sub-accounts, net investment of FIIs as of Aug. 31, 2002, in Indian Securities Market, stood at US $ 14.95 Billion.
12. Availability of derivative products like index

futures, index options, individual stock futures and individual stock options. In only 2 years, this young market has shown spectacular growth.

13. Availability of internet trading.
14. Strict disclosure and accounting norms for the listed companies. Facility of book building in public offerings through a transparent price discovery mechanism is available to the issuers.
15. Availability of Electronic Data Information Filing and Retrieval System (EDIFAR) for filing the corporate information and retrieval of the same by the stake-holders.
16. Implementation of Corporate Governance norms by way of the terms and conditions of listing agreement.

Despite the fact that Sebi has done a lot in the area of improving the functioning of capital market in India but still certain more steps are required to ensure a free and fair play of capital market in India. The seriousness with which Sebi is now trying to govern the capital market functioning gives an inkling about the back of mind status of this autonomous body. Some of the major priorities in future agenda (as recorded in the fact sheet of Sebi) include:

SETTING UP OF CENTRAL LISTING AUTHORITY (CLA)

- Corporatization and demutualization of stock exchanges.
- Strengthening of corporate governance through evaluation of form and measurement of wealth creation, wealth management and wealth sharing.
- Transition to T+2 rolling settlement by 2003 and T+1 by 2004.
- Improving liquidity through increased use of margin trading facility and securities lending.
- Setting up of investor Protection Corporation.
- Educating investors about the securities market.
- Strengthening risk management system for mutual funds.

- Expansion of product portfolio in derivative segment.
- Improving the quality of intermediaries and corporate governance at intermediaries.
- Strengthening regulatory transparency.
- Creation of market intelligence network and strengthening surveillance and enforcement.
- Development of active corporate bond market.
- Use of digital signatures in securities transactions.
- Development of self-regulatory organizations (SROs) in securities market.

In financial sector and capital market the stock exchanges have developed sophisticated institutional mechanisms making extensive use of modern computer technology. The mutual fund and insurance industries have also been opened to new private sector entry. The private sector market share in the mutual fund industry is now over 50 per cent. Further, US-64 scheme of UTI has been made NAV-based scheme.

Summing up, it could be said that the years 2000-03 has been difficult years for almost all economies of the world. World economic growth slowed down as did trade growth. Based on growth tendencies shown during closing of the year 2003 by the Indian economy and BSE Sensex hovering over 6000 mark, the signals are that recovery is expected in 2004 depending upon the political scenario after the elections.

GOVERNMENT REGULATION OF MUTUAL FUNDS AND THEIR PROSPECTS

On the other hand, after being bitten by capital market scams that emerged due to stock market irregularities, SEBI has been trying hard to control the markets. In this regard, continuous monitoring of markets and its players is done by the SEBI. It has also been issuing different circulars, notifications and guidelines for efficient and transparent working of stock markets. For improving mutual funds working in India, some important circulars issued in the year 1999 onwards by SEBI have been listed here below:

Year 1999

- Guidelines for participation by mutual funds in stock lending schemes.
- Investment in ADRs/GDRs by Mutual Funds.
- Reporting of transactions by Mutual Funds.

Year 2000

- AMFI recommendations for improving Disclosures and Compliance Standards—Frequency of Portfolio Disclosure, Formation of Audit and Valuation Committee.
- Guidelines for participation by Mutual Funds in Trading in Derivative Products.
- Payment of interest for delay in dispatch of redemption or repurchase proceeds.
- Guidelines for advertisement by Mutual Funds.
- Recording of Investment decisions by Mutual funds.

Year 2001

- Guidelines for updating of offer document, time frame for dispatch of dividend warrants and reporting of securities transactions by Directors of AMCs on Quarterly basis.
- Investment/Trading in Securities by Employees of Asset Management Companies.
- Putting Standard Observation on Website.
- Clients' Codes for Mutual Funds.
- Gazette Notification, Investments by Mutual Funds in Venture Capital Funds.
- Independent Directors on Boards of AMCs and Trustee Companies.

Year 2002

- Guidelines for Participation by Mutual Funds in Trading in Derivative Products.

- Registration of Intermediaries.
- Portfolio Disclosures.
- Calculation of sale and repurchase prices of units of Mutual Fund Scheme.
- Introduction of Benchmarks.

Year 2003

- Guidelines for Investments in Foreign Securities by Mutual Funds.
- Investment limits for government guaranteed debt securities.
- Minimum Number of Investors in Schemes/Plans of Mutual Funds.

Furthermore, SEBI Insider Trading Regulations-2002 has also been proposed to keep close surveillance on the working of mutual funds. The above-mentioned circulars and notifications show the back of the mind of this autonomous body. Though lately, it seems that SEBI has realized its responsibility of a watchdog for hard earnings of small Indian investors.

Another important aspect to be considered for assessing mutual fund industry's prospects in India is the role to be played by professional fund managers who can help sustain and grow mutual fund industry in the coming times. World over, including in India, drastic changes have occurred in the capital markets as regards information disclosures, reduced transaction costs and dematerialization of securities, specifically, leading to odd lot trading. This has resulted in a situation where individual investor with small investment can buy adequate number of securities of different companies and can build diversified portfolio of his choice (the function provided by mutual funds). Furthermore, dematerialization of securities lead to trading in odd lots, i.e. shares can be traded in fractions also. Shares of almost all companies are in dematting form thus leading to reduced costs, too. Moreover, any active investor can time the market because of information abundance and accuracy today. The chances of mispricing of securities in such type of market are remote.

Therefore, information availability for small investor is similar as for any fund manager. Thus, the survival of mutual funds and need for professional fund managers could be questioned. This could be answered briefly as:

1. All of the investors are not properly educated to understand the intricacies of financial figures published by different companies.
2. All shares have been covered under rolling settlements now thus making it difficult for a small investor to settle the account at every day end.
3. Flourishing mutual fund business hints at the small investor's belief in expertise of professional fund managers.

Also some reasons for these dependence traits of investors studied by behavioural economists have been summarized by Shashikant (1999) as below:

- Investors actually face an "S" shaped utility curve with lower tolerance for losses than gains. This means they would sell winning rather than losing stocks. Investors exhibit the preference to retain losers, thereby not rationally rebalancing their portfolios.
- Investors tend to overreact to positive information and are, therefore, prone to being influenced by fads. This is one of the important causes behind market bubbles.
- Investors are slow in updating their beliefs, and use their purchase prices as reference points in decision making. They are unable to tune their portfolios to the market price.

Thus the important role of professional fund managers emerges. Looking at the last year end performance of mutual funds, all equity funds and general investor in equity markets gained because of the Bull Run. (see Table 2) The table shows that equity funds have comeback in a big way, thereby, putting more responsibility on the shoulders of mutual fund

Scheme Name	Category	1 year Return (%)
Tata Equity Opportunity Fund	Diversified Equity	166
HDFC Index Fund-Sensex Plus	Index Fund	73.18
Birla Equity Plan	Tax Plan	144.17
Alliance Basic Ind.—Growth	Sector Specific	139.51
HDFC Prudence Fund—Growth	Balanced	82.29
UTI RBUP	Debt	26.97
FT India Gilt Invest. Plan	Gilt	20.79
Chola Liq. Institutional Fund	Liquid-MMMF	7.21

managers to provide a safe regime with handsome returns to the mutual fund investors in this volatile bullish capital markets.

The parliament was dissolved for conducting fresh elections on Feb. 6, 2004. That reign the galloping bull temporarily and the markets have gone volatile. In such tricky situations of falling markets all rests upon fund manager's market timing ability that how quickly the manager encash the equity investments and transfer the money to cash securities temporarily? This is not possible for a small investor.

The analysts, however, recommend that investors with minimum investible funds of Rs. 4-5 lacs should enter equity stock investment at this juncture, which is not possible for majority of small investors. Hence, only way out for them will be to enter enroute mutual funds. Therefore, professional fund managers have to shoulder the responsibility of safe investment on behalf of small investors.

The budget 2002-03 reimposed tax on income to be received by investors from mutual funds. Dividend income from equity-oriented schemes was to be taxed at a concessional rate of 10% for one more year. Interim Budget 2004-05 proposed to extend the concessions for not taxing the capital gains on equity shares acquired after March 31, 2003 by another three years. So, equity-oriented schemes will benefit as investors will prefer to go for growth funds.

One USA-based California Public Employees' Retirement System (CalPERS), the world's largest pension fund that manages assets to the tune of $ 159 bn has initiated a new permissible country review mechanism so as to decide the 'investibility of different countries based on certain parameters like Political Stability, Transparency, Productive Labour Practices, Market Liquidity and Volatility, Market Regulation/Legal System/Investor Protection, Capital Market Openness, Settlement Proficiency and Transaction Costs. As per the review India along with some other countries have been rated in the category of "unacceptable investment destination." But, however, the creditability of parameter rating by the said fund has been challenged by Donald L. Huskin, Chief Investment Officer, Trend Macrolytics, USA, "A fiduciary like CalPERS acting as a trustee to maximize the wealth of pension plan beneficiaries, has no place making judgments about political matters such as human rights, environmental responsibility etc."

PROSPECTS

From the foregoing discussion, five major aspects that would be helpful in assessing the future prospects of mutual funds in India are listed as:

1. Investors responses to the survey.
   (The results of the major study conducted by the author)
2. Economic growth parameters.
3. Government regulation of mutual funds.
4. Role of professional fund managers.

In nutshell, compiling these one by one precisely, it could be said that:

1. Though half of the existing investors in the survey have decided to opt out of the mutual funds, other half still wants to continue with their investments in mutual funds. Also, about 20% of investors surveyed fall in the category of new comers interested for making fresh investment in mutual funds. No doubt, the experience as regards returns

on investment from mutual funds of majority of investors has been shaky, but the role of SEBI and the management of the funds by professional managers, too, have been equally criticized. (This analysis from the study has been corroborated by the report of Joint Parliamentary Committee (JPC) in *Financial Express*, July 10, 2002 on front page confirming the mismanagement of capital markets by SEBI and other regulatory bodies like RBI and Finance Ministry). Overall, responses of the investors have been mixed.

2. As already discussed in this chapter, the growth potential of an Indian economy cannot be denied. Cyclic movements, however, could not be ruled out. Hence, growth pattern of different economic sectors looks positive; therefore, mutual funds industry is also expected to gain.
3. SEBI and other controlling bodies of capital markets have started monitoring the market movements more closely. A consistent effort is being made by them to refine the working of capital markets and mutual funds. This is expected to go a long way in reviving the lost confidence of small investors in mutual funds.
4. Last but not the least, the managers of these mutual funds needs to sharpen their skills further so to manage the pooled money in a total professional way. Market timing, during both the bull and the bear run, is the sole factor that would ensure their long-term survival in the trade.

In nutshell, it could be said that mutual funds invest their funds in stock markets, which in turn depends upon the economic performance and political stability of that economy on one hand and fund's professional management on the other. Hence, with flourishing business of mutual funds in India, conducive environment for capital markets expected to be provided by the government and positive initiatives being taken by SEBI to streamline mutual funds business, all now rests upon the professional fund managers that how they sharpen their market timing skills and diversify product range so to make funds tailor made to the needs of every investor to provide handsome returns to them who entrust their hard earned money to the fund managers.

References

Shashikant, Uma (1999), "Equity Investing, Investors and Mutual Funds," A paper presented at FICCI-UTI-ICM, July 27.

Sethu, G (1999), "The Mutual Fund Puzzle", A paper presented at UTI-ICM, December 23-24.

The Market Bureau Report (2002), "MF Investments Cross Rs 1,00,000 Crore", *The Financial Express*, August 13, p. 1.

Rashmi Das (2002), "Inactivity of FinMin, Sebi, RBI *et. al.* Led to Stock Scam: JPC", *The Financial Express*, July 10, 2002, p. 1.

Prasuna, D.G. (2002), "Emerging Markets Investors beware", *Chartered Financial Analyst*, April, pp. 35-38.

Tenth Anniversary Issue (2002), "Where we have been; What lies ahead", Business Today, Jan.

Jayakar, Roshni (2002), "Debt Be Not Proud, Equity's Back", *Business Today*, April, p. 43.

Jayakar, Roshni (2002), "The Mutual Funds Boom", *Business Today*, January, p. 69.

Jayakar, Roshni (2002), "BSE: Then And Now", *Business Today*, January, p. 63.

www.sebi.com
www.finmin.nic.in
www.rbi.org.in
www.amfi.com

12

Perception of Investors Regarding Financial Derivatives

REKHA HANDA

Financial innovation, internationalisation and institutionalisation of investment activities are different but ultimately inseparable aspects of the radical fundamental changes in the financial sector. The relentless pace of liberalisation and integration of Indian economy into the global economy has led to the discarding of traditional ways of working and imbibing innovations. It is the stock markets, in particular which have witnessed tremendous financial, technical and behavioural changes over the last two decades. Among these radical adjustments and innovations was the arrival of 'DERIVATIVES'.

History of financial markets is replete with crises, such as the break down of the Bretton Woods system of fixed exchange rate in 1971, the steep fall in the Nikkei in 1989 and the bond debacle of 1994 in US. It was because of very high degree of volatility of financial markets and their unpredictability. With the global integration of markets these disasters became more frequent. Investors and companies were exposed to uncontrollable casino-type forces and outcomes because products and financial markets had evolved into casinos. As a result, derivatives, innovative financial risk management instruments, took birth as saviors of the investors. It was expected that the introduction of derivatives will fuel the growth of the Indian capital markets. Derivatives were introduced to allow market participants, through a wide range of products, a facility for managing their risk exposures in a cost efficient way.

Derivatives or derivative securities are contracts which are written between two parties (counter parties) and whose value is derived from the value of underlying widely-held and easily marketable assets such as agricultural and other physical (tangible) commodities or currencies or short-term and long-term financial instruments or intangible things like commodities price index (inflation rate), equity price index or bond price index. The price of a derivative instrument is contingent on the value of its underlying asset. Accordingly, derivatives are also sometimes called contingent claims. Derivatives are also known as "deferred delivery or deferred payment instruments."

Derivatives create tailor-made investments with pay-off pattern to match the investor's requirements. It is the customizing ability of derivatives that makes them popular in international transactions in particular, and also accounts for their explosive growth in recent times.

FINANCIAL DERIVATIVES: THE GENESIS

Although financial derivatives came into the spotlight along with growing instability in current markets during the past-1970 period, the general concept has existed around the world for years. In case of India as well, options of various kinds (called *Teji* and *Mandi* and *Phatak*) in unorganized markets were traded as early as 1900 in Mumbai. Insurance products are one of the most prominent and widely used derivative instruments, although they were never introduced in the form of 'derivatives'.

The first step towards re-introduction of derivatives trading in India was the promulgation of the Securities Laws (Ammendment) Ordinance, 1995 that withdrew the prohibition on options put by the Securities and Contracts

Regulation Act (SCRA) in 1956. The real push to derivatives market was given by SEBI in November, 1996 by setting up a committee under the chairmanship of Dr. L.C. Gupta to develop, "appropriate regulatory framework for derivatives trading in India." The Securities Laws (Amendment in SCRA) Bill, 1999 was introduced to bring about the much-needed changes. In December 1999, the new framework was approved. Derivatives have since then been accorded the status of 'Securities'.

Introduction of derivatives was made in a phased manner allowing investors and traders sufficient time to get used to the new financial instruments. Index futures on CNX Nifty and BSE Sensex were introduced during 2000 and after a lag of about six months, index options and stock options were introduced. Though individual stock futures were considered highly risky even by US standards, SEBI permitted the Indian stock exchanges to trade on single index futures on 31 Indian stocks during 2001. The list has been increased to 53 scrips in 2003.

NEED OF THE STUDY

An individual investor is an important component of the financial markets, especially in India. The Indian investors were reeling under the ordeal of the Ketan Parekh scam and the subsequent meltdown of technology stocks, another bombshell jolted the markets in the form of UTI. The retail investor had been shattered and their confidence in the market was eroded significantly. SEBI, then, rolled out a plethora of pro-active measures, introduction of derivatives on stock exchanges being one of them.

In the present scenario when derivatives have taken the markets by a sweep, it is essential to study and analyze what the investor, who actually deals in them, feels about these financial derivatives. What are his expectations, apprehensions and interpretations about the derivatives? It is also essential to see how far those who are to actually deal in them have accepted these derivatives.

Hence, the need of this study.

RESEARCH METHODOLOGY

A number of studies have been and are being conducted in relation to derivatives and the associated aspects. The studies, however, have ignored the investor's viewpoint, the investor who is to actually deal in these financial instruments. The present study is a genuine step in this direction to explore the views and psychological disposition of a common investor with regards to financial derivatives. Their notions and perceptions, expectations and fears in relation to derivatives are tried to be studied.

The basic objective of this paper is to study and analyze the perceptions of the common investor about the financial derivatives. The study is directed towards specifically examining:

- Demographic characteristics and investment behaviour of those already dealing in or intending to deal in derivatives..
- The expectations and underlying fears of the common investor with regards to derivatives.
- The level of awareness of investors regarding derivatives and information sources relied on.
- The loopholes that need to be plugged in an appropriate manner to make derivatives trading more effective.

The universe for this study consisted of investors who are familiar with and have heard of financial derivatives—those who are not alien to this latest financial instrument. The sample size of the study is 70 investors (respondents) covering the cities of Ludhiana, Jalandhar and Amritsar, picked up through the technique of convenient and purposive sampling as the others could not be used due to the limitations of the study. The primary data so required has been collected through carefully designed questionnaire consisting basically of all close-ended questions for the ease of the respondents. The data collected through questionnaire has been analyzed with the help of mathematical tools like percentage and statistical techniques like chi-square test and factor analysis.

DATA ANALYSIS

The information gathered is intended to highlight the following aspects:

1. Investment Avenue opted.
2. Objective of investment.
3. Awareness about derivatives.
4. Dealing in/intention to deal in derivatives.
5. Sources of information.
6. Choice of type of derivatives.
7. Investment experience.
8. Opinion on various notions about derivatives.

I. Investment Avenue Opted

The table below shows the responses of the respondents regarding the avenues where they made their investment at present and which they would opt for in future.

The present investors of derivatives amount to a

TABLE I

Showing Investment Avenues Opted by the Respondents

Investment Avenues	*At present*		*In future*	
Bank deposits	46	(65.7%)	36	(51.4%)
PO Schemes	44	(62.8%)	37	(52.9%)
Mutual funds	24	(34.3%)	36	(51.4%)
Shares	57	(81.4%)	45	(64.3%)
Debentures/bonds	29	(41.4%)	24	(34.3%)
Jewellery	23	(32.9%)	20	(28.6%)
Derivatives	23	(32.9%)	41	(58.6%)
Any other (Real estate etc.)	5	(7.14%)	10	(14.3%)

* Figures in normal show the number of respondents.
** Figures in parenthesis show percentage of respondents.
*** Since one investor may invest in more than one avenue the percentage distributions will add up to more than 100.

notable percentage of 32.9% which shows that derivatives phenomenon is catching up with a common investor possibly due to the promises of risk transference, economy and convenience. Coming to the future investment patterns we see that the most popular remains the investment in shares. Investment in derivatives follows closely which highlights the strong potential of financial derivatives in the financial markets. Hence, shares are the most popular investment avenue and also great potential lies for derivatives markets in future as many investors have shown keen interest in this investment avenue.

2. Objective of Investment

The respondents were required to specify their objective of investment which would indicate the factors they look in for in an investment. The Table 2 below shows the respondents and their objective of investment.

TABLE 2

Showing the Objective of Investment of the Respondents

Objective of investment	*Number of respondents*	*Percentage of respondents*
Regular returns	17	24.29
Capital appreciation	6	8.57
Both	47	67.14
Total	70	100

The Table 2 illustrates that most of the respondents (67%) expect regular returns as well as capital appreciation from their investments. Individually each of these commands a low percentage showing a bent of mind towards a blend of both.

After this the association of this objective with the age, occupation and income of the respondent was checked using the chi-square test at 5% level of significance. Using the results of the chi-square test, it was concluded that the objective of investment is independent of the age and occupation but is significantly affected by the income of the respondent. The association cannot be ignored of objective and income calling for investment products to match the investor needs and income levels.

3. Awareness about Derivatives

The respondents were required to indicate whether or not they were aware of the recently introduced financial derivatives. The table below shows the tabulated results.

The Table 3 above makes it evident that 90% of the

TABLE 3

Showing Awareness about Derivatives among the Respondent

Aware	*No. of respondents*	*Percentage of respondents*
Yes	63	90
No	7	10
Total	70	100

investors are aware of and have heard of the financial derivatives signifying thereby that derivatives are known to an impressive majority of the investors and enjoy reasonable acceptability among the respondents.

Next, the awareness level for its association with the age, occupation and income of the respondent was checked using the chi-square test at 5% level of significance. The awareness of the respondents regarding derivatives was found to be statistically independent of their age. With regards to association with income and occupation the awareness level is dependent on them. This implies that nature of job and incomes earned have a significant impact on the awareness of the investor.

4. Dealing in Derivatives

The question required the investors to indicate if they deal in or intend to deal in derivatives. The responses have been tabulated in Table 4.

The Table 4 indicates that 77% of the respondents are already dealing in or intend to deal in derivatives in future. This highlights significant acceptability of the financial

TABLE 4

Showing Dealing/Intention to Deal in Derivatives among the Respondents

Intention	*Number of respondents*	*Percentage of respondents*
Yes	54	77.14
No	16	22.86
Total	70	100

derivatives by the individual investor.

On checking this variable for its association with age, occupation and income of the respondent using the chi-square test, we conclude that the dealings in derivatives or intentions to deal in derivatives are statistically independent of the age, occupation and income of the respondent. In other words, these demographic features of age, occupation and income do not affect the decision to deal in or abstain from dealing in derivatives.

5. Sources of Information

The respondents were required to indicate the sources on which they relied in making decision regarding derivatives. This was expected to indicate the popular, effective and reliable sources. The responses gathered are indicated in Table 5 on next page.

The table clearly indicates that the most popular sources of information with regard to derivatives, as indicated by the sample respondents, is newspapers and financial journals and magazines (62.9%). Thus, the investment decision involving derivatives (as indicated by sample) is significantly influenced by information contained in newspapers and financial journals and also the professional advice. This illustrates the reliability on sources which are comprehensive and extensive. Internet though being one of such sources is not that popular (though it is gradually picking up) even in this net age.

TABLE 5

Showing Sources of Information on which Respondents Rely

Source of information	*Number of respondents*	*Percentage of respondents*
Internet	25	35.7%
Financial journals	44	62.9%
Professional advice	41	58.6%
Friends/relatives	18	25.7%
Newspapers	44	62.9%
TV	30	42.9%

* Since one investor may rely on more than one source the percentage distributions will add up to more than 100.

6. Choice for Type of Derivatives

The respondents were required to tick the types of derivatives (of the given options) they had heard of to find which of the categories were more familiar to the common investors. The responses obtained are as below.

TABLE 6

Showing Types of Derivatives Known to the Respondents

Type of derivatives	Number of respondents	Percentage of respondents
Futures	66	94.3%
Options	61	87.4%
Swaps	11	15.7%
Weather derivatives	3	4.3%
Credit derivatives	5	7.1%
Captions	—	—
Swaptions	—	—

* Since one investor may be familiar with more than one type of derivatives the percentage distributions will add up to more than 100.

Table 6 above tabulation clearly highlights futures and options as the derivatives most familiar to the respondents. Where complex categories like captions and swaptions are completely unheard of and beyond comprehension, weather and credit derivatives are also little heard of.

7. Investment Experience

The respondents here were required to specify the time since when they have been investing in the stock market. The intention was to relate this to this experience with the dealing in derivatives.

TABLE 7

Showing Experience of Respondents on the Stock Markets

Investment experience	*No. of respondents*	*Percentage of respondents*
Less than 2 yrs.	9	12.86
2-5 yrs.	13	18.57
5-10 yrs.	27	38.57
More than 10 yrs.	21	30
Total	70	100

The Table 7 indicates that the investors investing in the various products traded on the stock exchanges have reasonable experience and a very low percentage of them are the new entrants. The tabulated data above leads us to the conclusion that the introduction of derivatives trading has not only captured investments of those already participating in the stock markets but also numerous investors who had so far been away from the stock exchanges and the products dealt therein.

8. Opinion on Various Notions about Derivatives

Here the respondents were presented with 'Likert Type' statements relating to different aspects of derivatives and were asked to rate them on a 5 point scale. For analysis of this part factor analysis has been done, required rotated factor matrix obtained and interpreted.

With the help of the factor analysis (eigen values, percentage of variance) eight factors as below are extracted. The percentage of total variance is used as an index to account how well the total factor solution accounts for what the variable together represent. The present solution accounts for 73.25% of total variance. This shows that the above model is satisfactory.

Naming of the Factors

All the factors extracted have been given appropriate names on the basis of variables represented in each case. The names of factors, the statements, labels and factors loadings have been summarized in the Table 8.

TABLE 8

Showing Statements with their Respective Factors

Factor No.	*Name of dimension*	*Label*	*Statement (Factor loading)*
1.	Important for capital market	X10	Derivatives are a defence against uncontrollable market forces (.764).
		X6	Derivatives have revived the sagging state of Indian stock market (.718)
		X4	Derivatives enhance volatility of short-term markets and funds (.651)
		X7	Derivatives enhance volatility of short-term markets and funds (.551).
2.	Ineffective control and lack of awareness	X8	The awareness and expertise of Indian investors and brokers needs to be improved (.803).
		X15	Need is of direct and active surveillance to prevent manipulations (.803)
		X13	Legal uncertainties and lack of clear instructions make derivatives confusing (.397).
3.	Lack of transparency and stability	X16	Efforts must be made to enhance transparency in dealing of derivatives (.765)
		X3	Political stability and stable economy are the main requisites of derivatives trading (.706).
		X17	Derivatives can be matched to investor requirements (.681).
4.	Level of risk	X14	Derivatives enhance the risk associated with future returns (.806).
		X18	Trading of derivatives on same exchanges is not healthy for their growth (.766).

5. Market efficiency	X5	Derivatives are ideal tools for speculation (.857).
	X1	Derivatives help to control fluctuations in stock prices (.564)
	X2	Derivatives trading enhance the efficiency of financial markets (.470).
6. Need of training and awareness	X12	Derivatives are double edged sword carrying danger of huge losses (.791).
	X20	Conducting workshops and educative seminars for investors can simplify the intricacies (.773).
7. Economical	X19	Derivatives trading is quick and cheap (.821).
8. Restricted growth	X9	Lack of liquidity and maturity in Indian markets restricts their steady growth (.839).
	X11	Derivatives do no create new profits only protect the existing ones (.437)

SUMMARY AND CONCLUSIONS

The Indian financial markets witnessed sweeping changes with the introduction of financial derivatives on the Indian bourses in June 2000. Initially the market witnessed low volumes being in the nascent stages of growth but this was expected to assume huge volumes with better understanding, increasing knowledge and acceptability of the instrument.

As was expected, with passing time the familiarity to this innovative instrument increased resulting in higher trading volumes and signs of revival in the markets which was followed by the ban on the traditional *badla* system.

The present project is a sincere effort to analyse the perceptions and associated fears of those actually dealing in and having first hand experience of the derivatives trading. The study was conducted with the objective of exploring the awareness level, investment experience and objectives of investment of the general investor. The preferred investment avenues of the investor with a special reference to the future prospects of developed and regulated derivatives trading was sought to be analysed through this study. Perceptions of institutional investors not being a part of the study and limited applicability of the results were the unavoidable limitations of the study.

In research methodology, convenient and purposive sampling techniques were adopted to draw a representative sample of 70 respondents for the study. Data was collected with the help of well-designed questionnaire and through various websites. After collection of the data it was tabulated and analysed by using simple percentages and statistical techniques like chi-square test and factor analysis, as and where required. On the basis of these results, interpretations were made and conclusions were drawn.

The prominent conclusions and findings of the study are outlined below:

- The popular investment avenues among the investors are shares, bank deposits and PO schemes.
- Derivatives as an investment avenue is the future investment channel of a significant percentage of respondents.
- Both regular returns as well as capital appreciation dominate as the objective of investment of the common investor.
- The objective of investment is significantly associated with the income of the respondent.
- The awareness about derivatives is statistically dependent on the occupation and income of the respondent but independent of his age.
- The intention to deal in derivatives is unaffected by the respondent's age, occupation and income.
- Newspapers, financial journals and magazines and professional advice are important sources of information which significantly influence the decision regarding derivatives.
- Futures and options are the only types of derivatives which command and understandability among the investors.
- Derivatives trading has attracted many new investors towards the stock markets.
- The importance for Capital Market has been

identified as the major factor related to derivatives. Derivatives are held as ideal tools for speculation by the investors as highlighted by the highest factor loading. The restricted growth is perceived as the factor lying last in importance.

The future of derivatives in India is very bright provided the trading is supported by strong and effective regulatory framework, guidelines on taxation and accounting of derivatives and high disciplinary and ethical working conditions.

DERIVATIVES: THE ROAD AHEAD

Trading in stock market derivatives has of course taken roots in the country and is on the growth path. A serious derivative market has emerged in a short span of time in India. A close look at the volume statistics pertaining to derivatives trading on Indian bourses leaves one wonderstruck. The turnover in the derivatives market has witnessed a sharp rise.

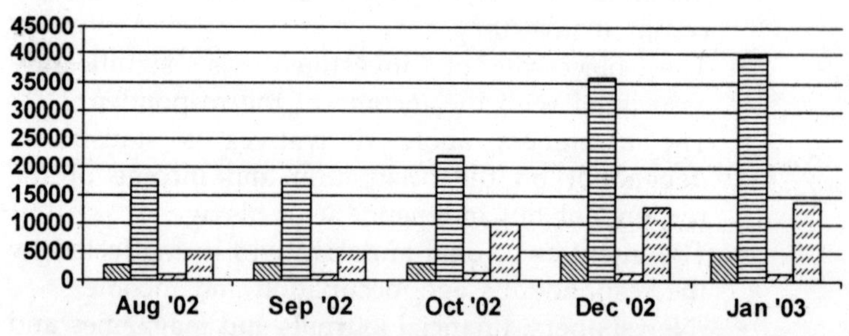

There are however certain irritants that need to be removed at the earliest if the market has to take deep roots quickly and smoothen the market volatility on the underlying assets. Some of the issues of concern which are crying for attention and immediate remedial steps include : the abnormally large lot size which till today keeps the hedging

Volume Statistics

Month	August 2002	September 2002	October 2002	November 2002	December 2002	January 2003
Index Futures	2,978	2,836	3,145	3,500	5,958	5,557
Stock Futures	17,881	17,501	21,213	25,463	35,532	38,299
Index Options	518	583	727	846	1,087	940
Stock Options	5,562	6,221	8,357	10,029	13,043	14,353
Total	26,939	27,141	33,442	39,838	55,620	59,149

Source: ww.nseindia.com.

facilities of derivatives out of the reach of ordinary investor, need to launch an awareness building campaign with a view to enhance confidence and knowledge among all market participants who till today find the derivatives market and the trading therein quite baffling, clearly outlining the legal framework so as to better answer the till date unanswered questions relating to taxation and accounting of derivatives, doing away with unreasonable margin requirements. The market is highly vocal in its argument that SEBI should design an effective monitoring, surveillance and risk management system at the level of the exchanges and clearing houses. These issues need to be addressed to realize the full potential of derivatives market. The derivatives failures world over, which keep haunting the investors have been due to inappropriate handling of these sophisticated instruments. It is the users who were the real culprits and not the instruments.

To conclude, derivatives have a great potential to rule and strengthen the Indian financial markets and acquire leading position globally provided the all underlying requisites are met and trading is done for the general good of the economy.

References

Aggarwal, A., "Derivatives: Wave of the Future (Indian Scenario)"; *Finance India,* Vol. XV, No. 2, June 2001, pp. 413-45.

Anantharaman, T.S., "Derivatives Option", *The Week,* May 31, 1998.

Bhole, L.M., "Financial Institutions and Markets: Structure Growth and Innovations"; Tata McGraw Hill Publishing Company Ltd., New Delhi, 2000.

Edwards, Charles, "Managing Derivatives Risk"; *Charted Secretary,* October 1998, pp. 989-91.

Ghosh, A., "Derivatives—Perfect Antidote to Casino-Effect", *Business Line,* July 20, 1998.

Hathaway, Kate, "Regulatory Parameters Associated with Successful Derivatives Markets", *Chartered Secretary,* October 1998, pp. 981-88.

Jayapandian, S., "Futures Trading: An Options Primer", *The Chartered Accountant,* May 1999, pp. 11-15.

Mayya, M.R., "Mutual Funds and Derivatives", *Business Standard,* March 17, 2000.

Somananthan, T.V., "Derivatives", Tata McGraw-Hill Publishing Company Ltd, New Delhi, 2001.

"Stock Market: How Smooth is the Transition", *Investment Monitor,* September, 2001, pp. 34-42.

"SEBI's Badla"; *Business India,* May 14-27, 2001, pp. 146-47.

Thiripalraju, M., K.M. Krishna and P. Naveen, "Futures with Futures", *The Merchant Banker Update,* November 1996, pp. 51-56.

Vaidyanathan, R., "Derivatives in the Indian Context—Need for Caution", *Chartered Secretary,* October 1998, pp. 1001-03.

Websites:

www.sebi.com

www.nseindia.com

www.bseindia.com

www.derivativesindia.com

13

Private Placement of Securities: Indian Experience

BALWINDER SINGH AND POOJA MALHOTRA

I. INTRODUCTION

The 1990s witnessed the emergence of the securities market as a major source of finance for trade and industry in India. A growing number of companies have been accessing the securities market rather than depending on loans from financial institutions (FIs)/banks. A Security market refers to as a mechanism for bringing together buyers and sellers of financial assets in order to facilitate trade. The securities market has two interdependent and inseparable segments, namely, primary market or new issues market and secondary market or stock market.

The primary market plays an important role in the securities market by forming a link between the savings and investments. It is through this market that the borrowers viz., the Government and the corporates, issue securities in which the investors deploy their savings. The primary market comprises, the public issues and the private placement market. A public issue consists of a company entering the market to raise funds from all types of investors; its debut is known as the Initial Public Offer (IPO). In case of private placement, there are only a few select subscribers to the issue. The securities can be issued at a face value, or at a discount/ premium; they may take a variety of forms such as equity, debt or some hybrid instrument. There are two major types of issuers of securities, the corporate entities who issue mainly debt and equity instruments and the government (central as well as state) who issue debt securities. These new securities issued in the primary market are traded in the secondary market.

The private placement market is an important source of long-term funds for Indian corporations. In particular, a private placement is a debt or equity security being issued in transactions "not involving any public offering." Companies (Amendment) Act, 2001 defines private placement, as an issue resulting in allotment to less than 50 persons.

The investors in this market conventionally are more sophisticated investors, such as banks, financial institutions (FIs), insurance companies, mutual funds, and high net worth individuals, generally referred to as qualified institutional buyers. The private placement issues are arranged by an intermediary like merchant banker or investment banker, who acts as an agent of the issuer and brings together the issuer and the investor(s). There are no mandatory disclosure and credit rating requirements for these issues. These issues also do not need registration with the regulatory authority. Listed companies as well as closely held private limited company can access the public through the private placement method. Through private placement equity shares, preference shares, cumulative convertible preference shares, debentures and bonds are sold. In India, private placement market is witnessing the introduction of several innovative debt market instruments such as step down/step-up debentures, liquid income debentures, bonds, etc.

1.1 Reasons for Dominance of Private Placement

The rationale for investing in the private placement market lies in the convenience and flexibility to the issuers as well as investors (Raju, *et. al.*, 2004). The major motives for the issuers to issue securities in private placement market are:

- Cost Effective
- Lesser Disclosure Requirements
- Suitable for all types of firms
- Convenient
- Time Effective
- Access Effective
- Structure Effectiveness
- Sale primarily to Institutional Investors
- Placement of all Types of Securities
- Rapid dismantling of shackles on institutional investments.
- Deregulation of economy.
- Subdued market of public issues.
- No mandatory lengthy issuance procedure
- No requirement of listing of bonds on stock exchange.
- Good supply of bonds at attractive rates.

2. PRIVATE PLACEMENT: TRENDS IN INDIAN SECURITIES MARKET

Private Placement has become a preferred means of raising resources by the corporate sector in India. In sharp contrast to a shrinking public issues market for corporate securities, the last few years have witnessed growing activity in the private placement market in India. An aggregate of Rs. 2,676,600 million were raised by the government and corporate sector during 2003-04 as against Rs. 2,572,201 million during the preceding year. Government raised about three fourth of the total resources, with central government alone raising nearly Rs. 1,476,360 million (nearly 55 percent).

Data in Table 13.1 shows that there is a high preference for raising resources in the primary market through private placement route. Private placements accounted for 89% of total resources mobilized through domestic issues by corporate sector during 2003-04 whereas it was just 30% in 1990-91.

After a long period of subdued activity, there were signs of revival in the public issues in 2003-04. This was due to the offers made by quality issuers evoking buoyant

TABLE 13.1

Resource Mobilization from the Primary Market

(Rs. mn.)

Issues	1990-91	1991-92	1992-93	1993-94	1994-95	1995-96	1996-97	1997-98	1998-99	1999-00	2000-01	2001-02	2002-03	2003-04
Corporate Securities	**142,190**	**163,660**	**235,370**	**444,980**	**480,840**	**366,890**	**371,470**	**421,250**	**601,920**	**724,500**	**783,956**	**744,032**	**752,411**	**695,030**
Domestic Issues	142,190	163,660	232,860	370,440	419,740	361,930	338,720	377,380	590,440	689,630	741,986	720,612	718,147	664,050
Public Issue	99,750	119,030	216,510	295,780	308,000	228,320	188,060	76,390	93,650	77,040	63,620	71,120	48,667	71,900
Non-Govt. Public Cos	43,120	61,930	198,030	193,300	264,170	160,750	104,100	31,380	50,130	51,530	48,900	56,920	18,777	32,100
PSU Bonds	56,630	57,100	10,620	55,860	30,700	22,920	33,940	29,820	—	—	—	—	—	—
Govt. Companies	—	—	4,300	8,190	8,880	10,000	6,500	430	—	—	—	3,500	—	1,000
Banks & FIs	—	—	3,560	38,430	4,250	34,650	43,520	14,760	43,520	25,510	14,720	10,700	29,890	38,800
Private Placement	42,440	44,630	16,350	74,660	111,740	133,610	150,660	300,990	496,790	612,590	678,360	649,500	669,480	592,150
Euro Issues	—	—	7,020	78,980	67,430	12,970	55,940	40,090	11,480	34,870	41,970	23,420	34,264	30,980
Government Securities	**115,580**	**122,840**	**176,900**	**545,330**	**432,310**	**467,830**	**426,880**	**673,860**	**1,060,670**	**1,133,360**	**1,284,830**	**1,525,080**	**1,819,790**	**1,981,570**
Central Government	89,890	89,190	138,850	503,880	381,080	405,090	361,520	596,370	939,530	996,300	1,151,830	1,338,010	1,511,260	1,476,360
State Governments	25,690	33,640	38,050	41,450	51,230	62,740	65,360	77,490	121,140	137,060	133,000	187,070	308,530	505,210
Total	**257,770**	**286,500**	**412,270**	**990,310**	**913,150**	**834,720**	**798,350**	**1,095,110**	**1,662,590**	**1,857,860**	**2,068,786**	**2,269,112**	**2,572,201**	**2,676,600**

Source: RBI Annual Report.

investors' interest (Table 13.1). In the private placement market, the SEBI, for the first time, imposed stringent disclosure norms in September 2003. As a result, the resources mobilized by way of private placement fell from 93.2% in 2002-03 to 89.2% of total domestic issues in 2003-04. The public issues mobilized Rs. 71,900 million during this year representing 10.8 percent of total domestic issues.

The trends in the issuance pattern of privately placed securities during the last couple of years are presented in Table 13.2 and Table 13.3, which reveal the following:

(i) The share of public sector in total private placement market is high as compared to private sector. The share of the private sector has also shown an increasing trend for the previous years.

(ii) The share of financial entities, both public and private has come down partly because of the limit imposed on raising of Tier 2 capital by banks.

(iii) Of late, there appears to be an increase in private placements by the private non-financial sector.

The tables provide the details of amount raised by financial institutions and non-financial institutions from private and public sector by way of private placement. From the table, it is clear that, private sector financial institutions have raised about 61.7 per cent of the total funds raised by private sector by way of private placement for the year 2003-04 as compared to 37.7 percent in the previous year. While the share of private sector non-financial institutions have come down from 62.3 percent in 2002-03 to 38.2 percent in 2003-04. Public sector financial and non-financial institutions have also shown the similar trend. Among the total funds raised through private placement market, the share of private sector has come down from 37.5 percent to 25.1 while the share of public sector has increased from 62.5 to 74.8 percent.

2.1 Private Placement of Debt

The private placement now entirely dominates the primary corporate market. Preferably funds are raised through private placement of debt instruments. According to

TABLE 13.2

Resource Mobilization in the Private Placement Market

(Rs. Crores)

Year	Private Sector			Public Sector			Grand Total
	Financial Institutions	Non-financial Institutions	Total	Financial Institutions	Non-financial Institutions	Total	
1995-96	2136	1934	4070	4552	4739	9291	13361
1996-97	1847	646	2493	6541	6032	12573	15066
1997-98	4323.7	4878.5	9202.2	9659.7	11236.7	20896.4	30098.6
1998-99	12174.2	4823.5	16997.7	20382.4	12298.9	32681.3	49679
1999-00	10875.2	8528.3	19403.5	17981.3	23874.2	41855.5	61259
2000-01	13262.6	9843	23105.6	26201.2	18529.6	44730.8	67836.4
2001-02	16019	12601	28620	17358	18898	36256	64876
2002-03	9454	15623	25077	20407	21464	41871	66948
2003-04	9178	5688	14866	25879	18470	44349	59215

Source: RBI.

TABLE 13.3

Resource Mobilization in the Private Placement Market

(in %)

Year	Private Sector			Public Sector		
	FIs (1/3)	Non-FIs (2/3)	Total (3/7)	FIs (4/6)	Non-FIs (5/6)	Total (6/7)
1995-96	52.48	47.52	30.46	48.99	51.01	69.54
1996-97	74.09	25.91	16.55	52.02	47.98	83.45
1997-98	46.99	53.01	30.57	46.23	53.77	69.43
1998-99	71.62	28.38	34.22	62.37	37.63	65.78
1999-00	56.05	43.95	31.67	42.96	57.04	68.33
2000-01	57.40	42.60	34.06	58.58	41.42	65.94
2001-02	55.97	44.03	44.11	47.88	52.12	55.89
2002-03	37.70	62.30	37.46	48.74	51.26	62.54
2003-04	61.74	38.26	25.11	58.35	41.65	74.89

Source: RBI.

Prime Database estimates (NSE, 2004), a total of 140 issuers (institutional and corporates) raised Rs. 484,279 million through 364 privately placed debt issues in 2003-04. 188 issues out of 364 were made by the public sector units, which together mobilized 87% of the total. The amount raised through the private placement of debt issues have been on an increasing trend over the past few years (Chart 13.1).

Mostly, debt securities were privately placed. Though, there were some instances of private placements of equity shares, there is no comprehensive data coverage of this. The two sources of information regarding private placement market in India are Prime Database and RBI. The former data set, however, pertains exclusively to debt issues. RBI data, which is compiled from information gathered from arrangers, covers equity private placements also.

RBI estimates the share of equity in total private placements as rather insignificant (NSE, 2004). Some idea, however, can be derived from the equity shares issued by NSE-listed companies on private placement basis. A total of 20 companies listed on NSE privately placed equities, mobilizing around Rs. 8,536 million during 2003-04 (Annexure 13.1).

Of the 364 debt private placements, 188 (52%) were from the government/banking sector that together mobilized 87% of the total amount mobilized. The All India Financial Institutions (AIFIs) and Banks continued to top the list with 52.3% (Rs. 253,088 million), followed by the State Level Undertakings with 13.5% share (Rs. 65,642 million) (Table 13.4). The top '10' issuers accounted for 41.2% of total private placement during 2003-04 (NSE, 2004).

Sectoral distribution shows that the financial sector continued to dominate the private placement market, raising 67% in 2003-04 followed by power sector, which accounted for 17% during the year (Table 13.5).

Unlike public issues of bonds, it is not mandatory for corporates issuing bonds in the private placement market to obtain and disclose credit rating from an approved credit rating agency. Rating is, however, required for listing. Of the 364 debt private placement deals during 2003-04, 328 issues (90%) went for rating and 36 did not get rated.

Chart 13.1

Growth of Private Placement of Debt

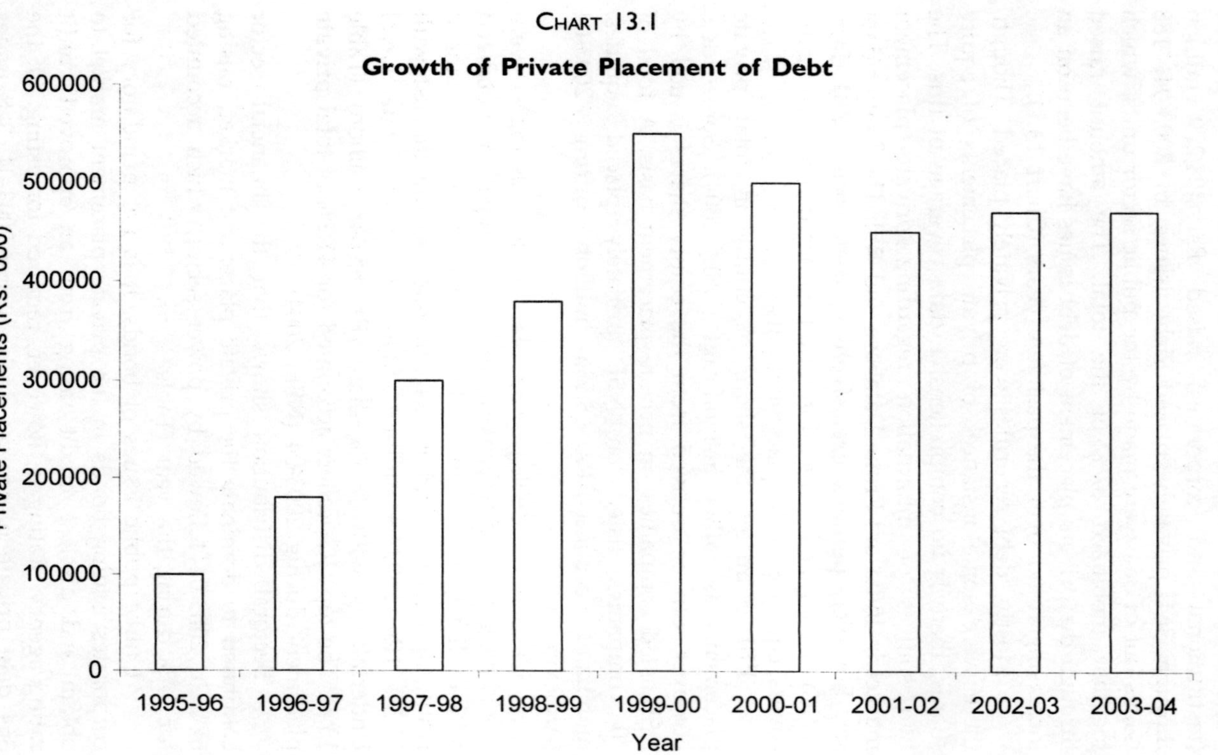

TABLE 13.4

Issuer-wise Distribution of Private Placement of Debt

Issuer	*Issue Amount (Rs. mn.)*		*% of Issue Amount*	
	2002-03	*2003-04*	*2002-03*	*2003-04*
All India Financial Institutions/Banks	173687	253088	35.87	52.26
State Financial Institutions	38665.2	42084	7.98	8.69
Public Sector Undertakings	125491	58809	25.92	12.14
State Level Undertakings	43894	65642	9.06	13.55
Private Sector	102498	64456	21.17	13.35
Total	484236	484279	100.0	100.0

Source: NSE, 2004.

TABLE 13.5

Sectoral Distribution of Resources Mobilized by Private Placement

(In percent)

Sector	*2002-03*	*2003-04*
Financial	50	67
Power	16	17
Water Resources	3	5
Telecommunications	1	1
Others	30	10
Total	100	100

Source: NSE, 2004.

The corporates have shown a preference for raising resources in the primary market through debt instruments as against equity and the major chunk of debt instruments is issued by way of private placements as against public issues (Table 13.6).

During 2003-04, the corporates raised a total of Rs. 527,519 million through debt issues, of which Rs. 484,279 million through private placement and Rs. 43,240 million through public issues.

TABLE 13.6

Resources Raised by Corporate Sector

(Amount in Rs. mn.)

Year	Public Equity Issues	Debt Issues			Total Resource Mobilisation (2+5)	Share (%) of Private Placement		Share (%) of Debt in total Resource Mobilisation (5/6*100)
		Public	Private Placements*	Total (3+4)		Total Debt (4/5*100)	Total Resource Mobilisation (4/6*100)	
1995-96	88820	29400	100350	129750	218570	77.34	45.91	59.36
1996-97	46710	69770	183910	253680	300390	72.50	61.22	84.45
1997-98	11320	19290	309830	329120	340450	94.14	91.01	96.67
1998-99	5040	74070	387480	461550	466580	83.95	83.05	98.92
1999-00	29750	46980	547010	593990	623740	92.09	87.70	95.23
2000-01	24790	41390	524335	565725	590520	92.68	88.79	95.80
2001-02	10820	53410	462220	515610	526430	89.64	87.80	97.94
2002-03	10390	46930	484236	561166	541556	91.16	89.42	98.08
2003-04	178210	43240	484279	527519	705729	91.80	68.62	74.75

* Data from 2000-01 onwards include only issues with a tenor and put/call option of 1 year or more, while data for earlier years include all privately placed debt issues irrespective of tenor.

** Provisional.

*** Includes Offers for Sale.

Source: NSE, 2004.

The privately placed debt issues make up a bulk of total debt issuances by accounting for 91.8%. The share of debt in total collection had been increasing consistently over the years but witnessed a reversal in the trend and stood at 74.8% in 2003-04 (Table 13.6). Private placement accounted for 68.6% of total resources mobilized by the corporate sector from the primary market. The corresponding share of public issues was a meager 25.3%.

3. REGULATORY FRAMEWORK AND CONCERNS

While the Reserve Bank of India (RBI) regulates the issuance of government securities, corporate debt securities fall under the regulatory purview of Securities and Exchange Board of India (SEBI). Coordination with Securities and Exchange Board of India (SEBI) is ensured both at a policy level and at operational level. Currently, amongst other things, RBI and SEBI are working together to devise a regulating mechanism for the issuers of private placements that will address issues of quality, transparency, end-use of funds and listing of such bonds.

Though, private placement market now provides a substantial part of corporate finance in India, what appears to be missing is a comprehensive framework governing issue of securities in this segment. While some measures have been taken in the recent past aiming to bring some order of discipline in the private placement market, a number of concerns still exist. All the 23 stock exchanges in the country provide facility for trading in corporate debt instruments. The bulk of the corporate bonds, being privately placed, are, however, not listed on stock exchanges. Besides, banks, whose financial health is the responsibility of the central bank, have a large exposure to the corporate bond market with more than 80 per cent of such investments being in privately placed corporate securities. Activity in the secondary market is thus rather thin. One obvious reason for the tremendous growth of private placement market could be an attempt by issuers to avoid regulatory compliance, which is mandatory for public issues.

Under the law, the difference between private

placement and public issues lies in the fact that the latter invite applications from as many subscribers, while the subscriptions in the private placement are restricted to a limited few. However, there has not been any noticeable difference in the activity in the private placement market. Corporates manage to bypass this legal requirement by issuing the securities to less than 50 persons in the initial stage and then sell these securities to a much larger number of investors.

The foremost concern in the private placement market is the quality of issues and extent of transparency in these deals. In the public issues, all the issues coming to the market are screened for their quality and the investors rely on ratings and other information for evaluation of risk. Such a screening mechanism is missing in case of private placements. This increases the risk associated with privately placed issues.

Many issues in the private placement market are made by public enterprises and often carry government guarantee as an element of security. However, a very little track of the end-use of funds is kept. These issues can be a potential threat to the financial system because of likelihood of their turning non-performing assets in the absence of adequate attention being paid to the continued viability of projects.

The default risk to investors could be a potential problem with private placements and may pose systemic risks if the subscribers to the issue happen to be large FIs. In the absence of standardized disclosure requirements, credit rating is one way by which the investors can assess the risk before taking an investment decision. In the private placement market, however, it is not mandatory to obtain rating on debt instruments, even though some issues are accompanied by rating. The issuer is also not required to make fair disclosure of all the credit ratings obtained.

While some privately placed issues are listed on stock exchanges, most of these are not. This implies that investors do not have an exit route if the business prospects of the corporates undergo a change. Listing of privately placed issues is not desirable without a minimum lock in period and if these securities are listed, they should be subject to same level of discipline as public issues are subjected to.

Another area, which needs to be explored, further is the investor pattern in the private placement market. In India, FIs/banks are the major issuers of privately placed debt. However, in the absence of data, it is difficult to judge the extent of exposure of different institutions to the private placement market. Some attempts should be made to develop a database in this regard.

To summarize, the core issue regarding private placements is insufficient disclosures. In the absence of regulatory provisions for disclosures, the institutional investors must insist on minimum disclosures and take steps to screen the issues. The regulatory decree is, however, necessary to put in place uniform practices in this regard and ensure that disclosures are detailed and fair. In order to ensure development of private placement market in a healthy manner, it is essential to lay down a clear policy framework for this segment.

3.1 Recent Initiatives by RBI and SEBI

The regulation of the private placement market has remained a nucleus issue of the policy-makers for last couple of years. However, there has not been much progress. As the non-transparent practices in this market is a matter of concern. In June 2001, RBI issued guidelines to investing banks on non-SLR investments, a substantial proportion of which is investment in privately placed securities. The guidelines cover prudential limits on investments, due diligence to be undertaken, the disclosures to be obtained, credit risk analysis of investment proposals, and internal rating of unrated issues. Subsequently a Working Group set-up by RBI (February 2002) went into the detailed disclosure norms and data collection measures on private placements.

3.2 Guidelines for Private Placement of Debt by Listed Companies

The Securities and Exchange Board of India (SEBI) has issued a circular on 30th September, 2003, to regulate the private placement of debt by listed companies, requiring them to comply with the following norms for private placement:

1. The company shall make full disclosures (initial and continuing) in the manner prescribed in Schedule II of the Companies Act, 1956, SEBI (Disclosure and Investor Protection) Guidelines, 2000 and the Listing Agreement with the exchanges. However, if the privately placed debt securities are in standard denomination of Rs. 10 lakhs, such disclosures may be made only through web sites of the Stock Exchange/s where the debt securities are sought to be listed.
2. The debt securities shall carry a credit rating of not less than investment grade from a Credit Rating Agency registered with the Board.
3. The company shall appoint SEBI registered Debenture Trustees in respect of the issue of the debt securities.
4. The debt securities shall be issued and traded in demat form.
5. The company shall sign a separate listing agreement with the exchange in respect of debt securities and comply with the conditions of listing.
6. All trades, except spot transactions between the two investors directly, in a listed debt security shall be executed only on the trading platform of an exchange.
7. The trading in privately placed debts will be only between Qualified Institutional Investors (QIBs) and High Networth Individuals (HNIs), where the standard denomination is Rs.10 lakhs.
8. SEBI registered intermediaries would be allowed to associate with privately placed unlisted debt issues and shall be responsible/accountable for such issues. SEBI registered intermediaries shall be required to furnish periodical reports to SEBI in this regard.
9. The requirement of Rule 19(2)(b) of the Securities Contract (Regulation) Rules, 1957 shall not be applicable to listing of privately placed debt securities on exchanges, subject to the condition that all the above requirements are complied with.

It is also clarified that if an investor is alloted securities of Rs. 1 lakh or less, such securities may be issued in physical form at the option of the investor. The trading in the privately placed debt securities would be permitted in standard denomination of Rs. 10 lakhs in the anonymous, order driven system of the stock exchanges in a separate trading segment.

4. CONCLUSIONS

Private placement of securities is an accepted practice world-wide due to transactional advantages offered through the use of this route. Benefits include a lower cost of borrowing, by avoiding costs associated with disclosure and advertisement, and the ability to borrow at one go, rather than access markets in trenches with their associated repeated transaction costs, without adverse effects on prices. In India, additionally, the peculiarities of its financial regulations confer another benefit to banks in subscribing to debt issues, whether public or private: exemption of placements from priority sector lending requirements, which are applicable in the event of direct loans (credit). However, these benefits depend upon the efficiency of this market. This paper is an attempt to study a few aspects of efficiency of private placement market in India by reviewing the past developments and helps to identify the weaknesses/gaps in this segment. Major findings of the study are:

1. The private placement now entirely dominates the primary corporate market. Private placements accounted for 89% of total resources mobilized through domestic issues by corporate sector during 2003-04 whereas it was just 30% in 1990-91.
2. In the private placement market, the SEBI, for the first time, imposed stringent disclosure norms in September 2003. As a result, the resources mobilized by Non-government entities fell from 93.2% in 2002-03 to 89% in 2003-04.
3. Mostly, securities issued in the private placement market are debt securities. The amount raised

through the private placement of debt issues have been on an increasing trend over the past few years. Though there are some instances of private placements of equity shares. Around Rs. 4,400 crores worth of such equity shares were listed on NSE during 2000-01. This indicates that equity private placement may not be that small an amount.

4. The private placement market in India is largely dominated by public sector entities, including All India Financial Institutions (AIFIs). AIFIs and banks led with 52.3 per cent, followed by the State Level Undertakings with 13.5% share during 2003-04.
5. Analyzing the industry-wise data, the financial sector dominates the private placement market. It accounted for 67 per cent of total resource mobilization through the private placement route during 2003-04. This was followed by the power sector with shares of 17 per cent.
6. The private placement market appears to be quite concentrated among a few issuers. The top 10 issuers accounted for 41.2% of total private placement during 2003-04. Their corresponding share for April-September 2001 was 42.5 per cent. It may be noted that two FIs, viz. ICICI and IDBI, together mobilized 17 per cent of total resources mobilized by way of private placement during April-September, 2001.
7. Unlike public issues of bonds, it is not mandatory for corporates issuing bonds in the private placement market to obtain and disclose credit rating from an approved credit rating agency, though many issues do carry rating. Rating is, however, required for listing. Of the 364 debt private placement deals during 2003-04, 328 issues (90%) went for rating and 36 did not get rated or the rating information was not available.
8. On the investor side, the major subscribers in the private placement market in India are the FIs, banks, mutual funds, and insurance companies. However, there is no data available to enable one

to analyze the exposure of different entities to privately placed issues.

The core issue regarding private placements is insufficient disclosures. Disclosure should be made mandatory irrespective of the number of subscribers. Recently disclosures have been made compulsory for all listed companies coming out with private placement. If an unlisted company wants to come out with a private placement and intends to get it listed, disclosures have been again made mandatory. However, the unlisted companies who do not fall under the jurisdiction of SEBI still are free to make private placement without adequate disclosures. This needs to be plugged with the help of respective regulatory bodies or by expanding the jurisdiction of SEBI. In order to ensure development of private placement market in a healthy manner, it is essential to lay down a clear policy framework for this segment.

Private placement of debt should be encouraged subject to the following conditions:

- All privately placed debt will be issued to qualified institutional investors as well as to other institutions but not to the retail investors.
- All private placements will be carried out by debt manager and/or primary dealer.
- All private placements will be compulsorily admitted for listing and regular information should be made available as specified previously.

To conclude, though private placement method being—less complex, less expensive, more convenient with lesser disclosure requirements, has its own merits. Yet it has to go a long way to become an investor trusted source of raising funds.

References

Datar, M.K. (2001), "Private Placements: Market or Institution?" Paper Presented at The Fifth Capital Market Conference, December 20-21.

Hajra, K.S. (2001), "Private Placement Market" *NSE News*, October.

NSE (2004), *Indian Securities Market: A Review,* Vol. VII.

Raju, M.T., Bhutani, U. and Sahay, A. (2004), "Corporate Debt Market in India: Key Issues and Some Policy Recommendations," *Working Paper,* No. 9, SEBI, July.

Reserve Bank of India (various): *Annual Reports.*

Reserve Bank of India (various): *Report on Currency and Finance.*

Reserve Bank of India (various): *Statement on Monetary and Credit Policy.*

Shirai, S. (2004), "Impact of Financial and Capital Market Reforms on Corporate Finance in India," *Asia-Pacific Development Journal,* Vol. 11, No. 2, December.

ANNEXURE 13.1

Details of Private Placement Issues by NSE-listed Companies during the period April 1, 2003 to March 31, 2004 and listed on the Capital Market Segment of the Exchange

Sl. No.	Name of Company	Number of Securities	Funds Raised (Rs. lakh)	Face Value (Rs.)	Issue Price (Rs.)	Close Price as end-March 2004 (Rs.)
1.	Aurobindo Pharma Ltd.	1050000	2373	10	226.00	374.6
2.	Usha Beltron Ltd.	5264727	1737	5	33.00	37.80
3.	Usha Beltron Ltd.	5345455	1764	5	33.00	37.80
4.	The Dhampur Sugar Mills Ltd.	10000000	1000	10	10.00	24.50
5.	Padmalaya Telefilms Ltd.	2000000	2844	10	142.20	56.05
6.	UTI Bank Ltd.	38362834	16400	10	42.75	148.65
7.	Nuchem Ltd.	2067130	207	10	10.00	1.95
8.	Arvind Mills Ltd.	146033	22	10	15.00	45.55
9.	Arvind Mills Ltd.	63949	10	10	15.00	45.55
10.	Arvind Mills Ltd.	7776489	1166	10	15.00	45.55
11.	Arvind Mills Ltd.	1551796	233	10	15.00	45.55
12.	Arvind Mills Ltd.	7350000	1103	10	15.00	45.55
13.	Khandwala Securities Ltd.	120000	26	10	22.00	9.05
14.	Strides Acrolab Ltd.	3144445	3144	10	100.00	—
15.	Orchid Chemicals & Pharmaceuticals Ltd.	4382727	9642	10	220.00	200.15
16.	Pantaloon Retail (India) Ltd.	865000	433	10	50.00	288.65
17.	Jindal Vijayanagar Steel Ltd.**	279034907	27903	10	10.00	8.20
18.	Shriram Transport Finance Co. Ltd.	6243000	749	10	12.00	—
19.	Strides Acrolab Ltd.	13714286	9600	10	70.00	—
20.	Glenmark Pharmaceuticals Ltd.	8185570	5000	2	61.08	143.70
		—	85356	—	—	—

** Indicates preference shares issued on preferential basis.
Source: NSE.

14

Risk Management

SAKSHI VASUDEVA

INTRODUCTION

There has been a significant change in the world economy in three respects in last twenty years. First, the advent of floating exchange rates has led to unprecedented volatility in interest rates and exchange rates. Second, the globalization of trade and finance, which led to increased integration of markets. Third that commodity prices have become unstable. About twenty-thirty years back, corporate managers in developed countries were concerned mainly with issues such as marketing strategy, production and inventory management, quality and cost control. They used to face risks largely related to production costs and behaviour of product markets. However, the advent of floating exchange rates and overall market liberalization has complicated the management of business and altered the nature of risk involved. That's why; the area of risk management has assumed special significance in light of the deregulation happening in the financial markets of emerging markets. Even in the economies where the deregulation and reforms in financial sector have taken off very recently, there is a need for well thought out and debated ideas to carry out this process smoothly.

MEANING AND SOURCES OF RISK

We cannot talk about risk management unless we know what do we mean by risk?

Risk is Uncertainty in Achieving Objectives

Risks are uncertain future events, which could influence the achievement of the organization's strategic, operational and financial goals. The dimensions of risk include the impact on an organization's reputation, even the loss from activities, which are not acceptable to the society.

There are various kinds of risk which are faced by a business:

(a) Unsystematic Risk

Unsystematic Risk is specific to particular company or an industry. Unsystematic risk is that portion of total risk that arises due to the factors which affects the internal working of the firm. The factors like, management capability, labour strikes and stages in product life cycle can result in the variability of firm's return. No doubt, it can be eliminated through diversification and proper asset allocation. An investor gets no reward for taking un-needed unsystematic risk as this risk can be easily eliminated by diversification.

(b) Systematic Risk

Two main sources of systematic risks are: business risk and financial risk

Business Risk

Business risk is faced by the firm due to the operating conditions prevailing within a firm and also the extent to which these conditions effects the operating income and expected dividend variability of the firm. Business risk can be divided into two categories: internal and external.

Internal Business Risk signifies the internal competency or efficiency of the firm to effectively operate in the environment imposed on it. Every business firm is faced with internal risks and the degree to which these risks are minimized depends on the efficiency of the firm. External

Business Risk arises from the circumstances in the operating environment, which are beyond the control of the firm. Every firm faces certain external risk, which arises as the result of operating in the specific industry.

Financial Risk

It constitutes the ways and means by which company finances their activity. The degree of financial risk could be inferred from the capital structure of a firm. The amount of debt or borrowed capital in the financial structure signifies interest payment by the firm to the debt holders or preference shareholders. As a result, the earning left for equity shareholders keeps varying depending on the interest and principal payments. Financial risk is avoidable to the extent to which the management has the freedom to decide whether to borrow money or not. A debt free firm bears no financial risk.

Only Systematic risk is priced and, hence, has an influence on the required rate of return. Since the price of systematic risk is identical for all the participants in the financial market, a firm does not benefit its shareholders by laying it off in the financial market. This argument implies that company specific risks (or unsystematic risks), as long as they do not jeopardize the existence of the firm, do not hurt the shareholders. Recent academic work, however, has questioned this view. Although unsystematic risk may not have any bearing on the required rate of return in the financial market, unmanaged unsystematic risk can and often does hurt shareholders. Other thing being equal, a firm with a high total risk exposure is likely to face financial difficulties, which tend to have a disrupting effect on the operating side of the business. A distressed financial condition is likely to: (i) result in the problem of adverse incentives, (ii) weaken the commitment of various stakeholders, and (iii) impair the ability of the firm to avail its tax shelters.

Sources of Risk

Exchange Rates, Interest Rates and Commodity Price Risk

The movement of exchange rates affects firms involved with international trade, as well as firms that have utilized international financing. Consider a company that financed new investment with a dollar loan. During the construction period local currency was devalued by more than 60% with the result that project costs increased more than 60% and company will not be able to pay back its international debt.

The changes in interest, either in local or international, can prove to be equally devastating if left undamaged. Regarding, Commodity Price Risk, which means unpredictable changes in the price of commodity. Take the case of Caribbean cotton growing project. At the time when project was proposed, international cotton prices were near an historic low. With good soils, skilled management and the possibility of two crops per year the project looked good in paper, even for prices 10% lower than those observed at the time and well below informed forecast. By the time the project came in life 3 years later, however international prices had dropped by over 40% following an increase in world production. The development made the project un-feasible, and after various attempts of revival the company went bankrupt.

There are other kinds of risk as well:

Insurable Risk

These are those risks that a firm can protect themselves against by paying an insurance premium. The insurance company than bears any resulting liabilities or cost of damages. The risks of this sort are often physical in nature and include fire, mechanical failure and other accidents.

Economic and Political Risk

It originates from the nature of economy and country in which firms do business. Inflation, economic growth rates, the BOP, country risk and regulation are included in it.

Inflation Risk

Inflation and its uncertainty both influence the financial planning of firms. High inflation is also volatile which induce firms to devote more resources to the task of financial management. It also forces firms to shorten their planning horizons. In such a highly inflationary situation, risk management becomes all the more important for the firm.

Economic Growth Rate and BOP

The higher growth rate may lead to a sense of optimism about the future, a perception that local currency will be strong and possibly a lower aversion to risk. But this indirectly reveals that management is often willing to accept higher level of exposure to risk than other vise. Similarly, a surplus in the current (or trade) account of BOP may instill a feeling of confidence in a currency that induces firms to bear more exchange risks than normal.

Country Risk

It is the combination of macro-economic and political factors upon which international markets base a credit assessment. The consequences of this risk are higher cost of funds and shorter maturities. This has important implication for risk managers because it can severely limit their assess to some important derivative securities, which have long maturities.

RISK MANAGEMENT TECHNIQUES

Before going for a discussion on various risk management tools, let us first try to probe the importance of risk management.

Risk management is integral to sustainable shareholder value creation. Risk management establishes, calibrates and realigns the relationship between risk, growth and return. The crux of financial risk management is to maintain sustainable growth in shareholder value linked to risk, which in turn drives value; but it is an interactive and a continuous process. We can't avoid the risk to full extent, but we can analyze the risk, characterizing future cash flows and if we found it at the adjustable rate we can go for it. Risk stems from uncertainty from future and profit is the reward of risk. Managing risk using modern financial instrument eliminates all uncertainties, including both favourable and unfavourable outcomes.

Hedging Risk

Identification of the risk is a prior condition to hedging. Once it has been identified, it can be quantified with probabilities and perhaps with simulations.

For example, if the sources of risk were interest rates, we would like to know what would be the value of the security with a change in interest rates. Hedging is taking a derivative position opposite to our exposure. Suppose you find that the returns of X and Y are perfectly correlated. To hedge, you need to buy X and sell Y or to do the other way. When you do this, your net position is risk less. The preference is for a perfect hedge, but this is not usually possible. This can be with future contracts, forward contracts, options or swaps forwards, future, swaps, options, etc.

Forward Contract

A forward contract is an agreement between two parties to exchange an asset for cash at a pre-determined future date for a price that is specified today.

Hedging with forward contract for e.g. if you agree on 1 January to buy 200 tons of cotton in April at a price "x" then you have entered into a forward contract with the cotton dealer. According to this agreement you have bought forward cotton or you are long forward cotton, whereas cotton dealer has sold forward cotton or is short forward cotton.

Short Position

It commits the seller to deliver an item at the contracted price on maturity.

Long Position

It commits the buyer to purchase the item at contracted price on maturity.

Pay-off Profile

What are pay-offs to the forward buyer and forward seller? When the spot price in future exceeds the contracted price, the forward buyer gains spot price-contract price. If it is other way then loss is contract price- spot price.

Pay-off Profile for a Forward Contract

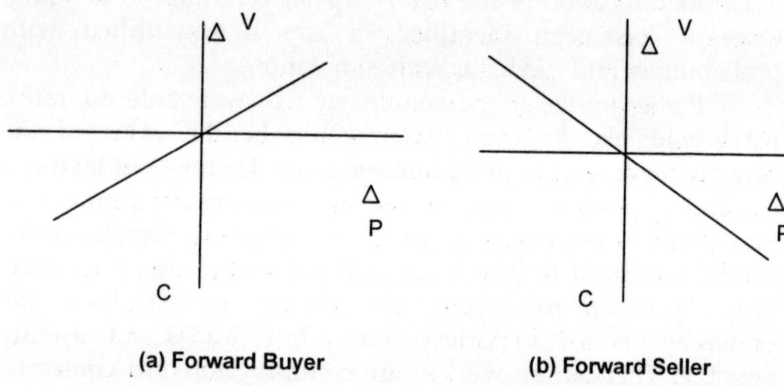

(a) Forward Buyer (b) Forward Seller

Pay-off to the seller of a forward contract is a mirror image of the pay-off to the buyer

How Forward Contract can be Used for Hedging?

For example, the changes in price of oil due to war, shortage or calamity are a source of risk for any country as it can completely change its economy. A country can do to cope with its oil price risk by buying a forward contract. If it does so its exposure to unexpected changes in oil prices will be eliminated.

Hedging with Future Contracts

A future contract is standardized forward contract. A forward contract is tailor made contract (terms are negotiated between buyer and seller) where a future contract is standardized contract (quantity, date and delivery condition are standardized).

How a Futures Contract is Different from Forward Contract?

A futures contract can be distinguished from a forward contract in the following ways:

- Futures contracts always trade on an organized exchange.
- Futures contracts have standardized terms. The terms of the contract are decided, when it would be fulfilled, and the condition of the product, etc.

  Forwards *vs.* Futures—Standardized Terms in Futures:

  (i) Quantity of the underlying ,

  (ii) Quality of the underlying (not required in financial futures),

  (iii) The date and month of delivery,

  (iv) The units of price quotation (not the price itself) and minimum change in price (tick-size), and

  (v) Location of Settlement, etc.
- Futures exchanges use clearinghouses to guarantee that the terms of the futures contract is fulfilled. The futures exchanges use clearinghouses to see to it that the obligations of the contract are fulfilled. The clearinghouse is the actual buyer of the contract from the short seller. And the clearinghouse is the actual seller of the long contract. If either party defaults on the contract the clearinghouse steps in and becomes the seller or buyer of last resort. The clearinghouse guarantees that the contract will be fulfilled. Neither party needs to trust the other party. In the history of futures trading in America, the clearinghouse system has always worked.
- Margins and daily settlement are required with futures trading. These are other safeguards in the futures market. Each customer must put up a good faith deposit. The amount of this margin varies from exchange to exchange and broker to broker. However, no broker may margin a contract for less than the exchange minimum. Each trading day every futures contract is assessed for liquidity. If the margin drops below a certain level the trader must deposit additional margin. This is called 'Maintenance Margin'.

Illustration: Suppose on April 1st, you take a long position in a future contract that matures on August 1st agreed upon price is, say, Rs. 100 at the close of trading on July 1st, future price rises to Rs. 105. The marking to market feature means that three things have been occurred—
First, you will receive a cash profit of Rs. 5. Second, the existing future contract with a price of Rs. 100 is cancelled. Third, you will receive a new future contract at Rs. 105.

- Futures positions can easily be closed. The trader has the option of taking physical deliver. Placing an off-setting trade and arranging an exchange-for-physicals transaction. The futures exchange makes exiting a contract relatively easy.
- Finally, forward contract markets are self-regulating and futures markets are regulated by certain agencies dedicated to this responsibility.

Broadly there are two types of futures—commodity futures and financial futures. A commodity futures is a futures contract in a commodity like cocoa or aluminum; a financial futures is a futures contract in a financial instrument such as treasury bill or currency.

The following relationship holds between the spot and futures prices for financial instruments.

$$\frac{\text{future prices}}{[1 + r_f]^t} = \text{present value of interest and divided}$$

payments foregone.

The following relationship holds for commodities.

$$\frac{\text{future prices}}{[1 + r_f]^t} = \text{spot price + present value of storage}$$

costs – present value of convenience yield.

Swaps

A swap basically involves and exchange of one set of financial obligations with another. The two most important kinds of financial swaps are the interest ıate swap and the currency swap.

An interest rate swap; is a transaction involving an exchange of one stream of interest obligations for another. Typically. It results in an exchange of fixed interest payments for floating rate interest payments.

Illustration: X has a borrowing of $ 100 million on which a floating interest rate of LIBOR (London inter-bank office rate) plus .25% is payable and Y has a borrowing of 100 million $ on which a fixed interest of 10.5% is payable X and Y enter into an interest rate swamp transaction under which X agrees to pay Y a fixed interest of 10.5% and Y agrees to pay X a floating interest rate of LIBOR plus .25%.

Diagrammatically represented as :

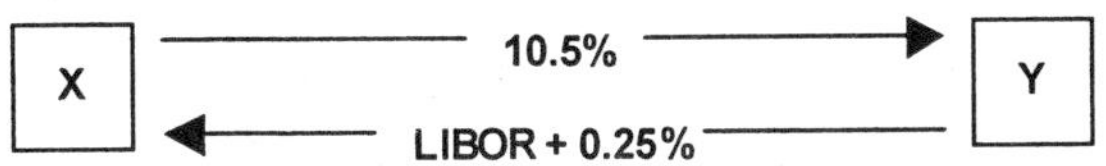

Floating rate borrowing

Fixed rate borrowing

Currency Swaps

In a currency swap both the principal and interest in one currency are swaped for principal and interest in another currency. On maturity principal amounts are swaped back.

Thus the currency swap involves:

1. An exchange of principal amounts today.
2. An exchange interest payment during the currency of the loan.
3. An exchange of principal amounts at the time of maturity.

Swaps may be induced by the following factors spread compression, market segmentation, market saturation, and difference in financial norms.

Hedging with Option Contracts

An option contract is an agreement under which the seller (or writer) of the option grants the buyer (or holder) the right, but not the obligation, to buy or sell (depending on whether it is a call option or a put option) some asset at a predetermined price during a specified period. The buyer (or holder) of an option has to pay the premium to enjoy the right. An option on an asset gives the buyer the right to buy or sell, the underlying asset at a fixed price over a fixed period of time.

There are a variety of option types. Put option give the right to sell. Call options the right to buy. The seller is commonly referred as the writer of the option, while the price is callers the premium.

Options are sold both over-the-counter by financial institutions and on organized exchanges and are available for a variety of assets including many currencies, interest rate instruments and commodities. E.g., purchase of a put option on pounds combined with the simultaneous sale of a call option on pound combined with the simultaneous sale of a call option on pound produces what is known as a collar that sandwiches the future dollar exchange rate between two known values.

Option Pay-off Profiles

The following figure shows the pay-off profiles for call and put options. The horizontal axis shows the difference between the value of the asset and exercise price of the option; the vertical axis shows the pay-off from the options.

Part A shows pay-off profiles of call option from buyer's point of view. Part B shows the pay off profile of call option from seller's point of view. Part C shows pay-off profile for buyer of a put option. Remember that a put option gives it buyer, the right to sell an asset at the strike price. Hence, if the value of asset falls below strike price, the buyer

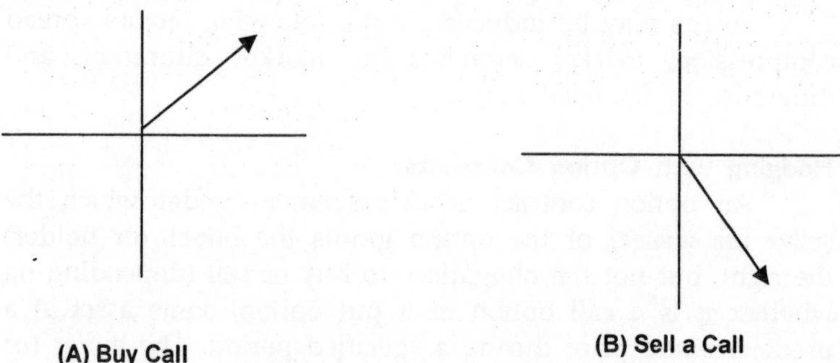

(A) Buy Call

(B) Sell a Call

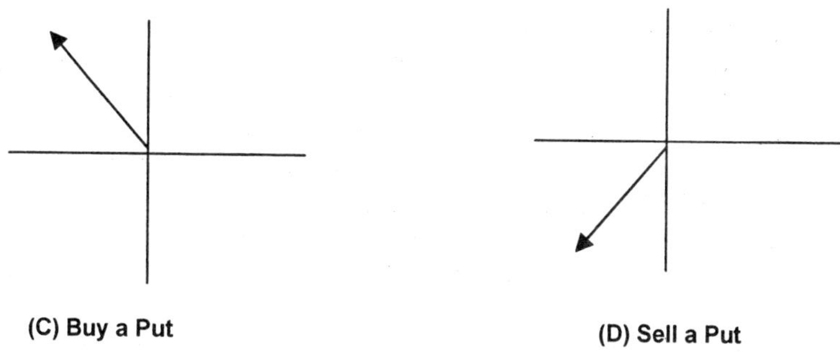

(C) Buy a Put (D) Sell a Put

profits because the seller of the put option is obliged to pay the strike price. Part D shows pay-off profiles for the seller of a put option.

GUIDELINES FOR RISK MANAGEMENT

In today's world managing corporate risks is a daunting task in coping with this challenge the following guidelines should be borne in mind:

(i) Align risk management with corporate strategy.
(ii) Proactively manage uncertainties.
(iii) Employ a mix of real and financial methods.
(iv) Know the limits of risk management tools.
(v) Do not put undue pressure on corporate treasuries to generate profits.
(vi) Learn when it is worth reducing risk.

A firm must carefully look at various risk management methods and select a judicious mix of the same. It appears that the financial often cost less than the real methods wherever there is scope for mutual substitution. The key guidelines to be followed in proactively managing uncertainly are as follows: (i) if you are confronted with a high level of uncertainty you need to employ greater flexibility, (ii) if you are confronted with a low level of uncertainty, you should pursue a focused strategy.

The corporate value is created primarily by making good investments (positive NPV investments). Hence, the over riding objective of risk management is to ensure that the company has the cash to support value enhancing investments. As external financing is often costly the risk management strategy of the firm should seeks to align the internal generation of funds to the demand for funds. In its risk management efforts a firm should know its risk bearing abilities. Its optimal level of risk, risk substitution possibilities, and risk reduction bargains. Financial engineering can be employed to solve complex business problems and advance corporate strategy. Enron capital and trade resources used financial engineering to bundle methane molecule with reliable deliveries and predictable prices that appealed to buyers. The Tennessee valley authority used call options on power for augmenting its capacity building power plants. (Chandra, Prasanna, 2003, Financial Management, pp. 1065-69)

It is well said by Cohen and Peacock, "Taking and managing risk is at heart of shareholder value ... creation. Yet current approaches to shareholder value creation often emphasize growth and return while paying little attention to specific risks inherent in implementing profitable growth strategies. Where risk is identified, many companies continue to rely on static financial risk mitigation strategies such as foreign exchange and capital structure practices formulated when the organization's size and structure were different. While the stock market has been rewarding companies for their success in creating shareholder's wealth, new approaches are necessary to sustain current levels of growth. A handful of companies are demonstrating that a more dynamic approach to risk management is critical to deliver superior performance, superior returns to shareholders. To this end the management must expand its approach to shareholder value by integrating a dynamic concept of risk into existing focus on growth and returns."

SUMMARY

Corporate financial risk management needs are increasingly related to operating performance and shareholder value enhancement, as well as compliance and prevention.

Financial risk is only a part (and, in many cases, a small part) of the risks carried by a company. The popular financial methods of risk management are: Forwards, futures, swaps, and options. The certain guidelines should be borne in mind while managing a financial risk.

References

Glen, Jack D. (1993), How firms in developing countries Manage Risk. International Finance Corporation.

Chandra, P. (2003), Financial Management, Tata McGraw-Hill Publishing Company Limited.

www.Globalrisksolution.com

www.indiainfoline.com

www.mentormanage.com

http://www.indiainfoline.com/bisc/rism.html

http://www.karvy.com/drvtives/forwards.htm

http://www.karvy.com/drvtives/swaps.htm

http://www.emecklai.com/mecklai/consulting/NTGEapproachtorisk.asps

15

Long-run Performance of IPOs in India

BALWINDER SINGH AND R.K. MITTAL

The long-term share price performance of Initial Public Offerings (IPOs) has recently become the focus of attention. It has been well documented since Stoll and Curley (1970), who observed that 'in the long-run, investors in small firms did not fare so well . . .' (pp. 314-15).

Summarising a wealth of international IPO evidence on the long-run performance of IPOs in a Table which has been reproduced below, Loughran, Ritter and Rydqvist (1994) reported that market adjusted 3-year abnormal performance following an IPO is always small and mostly negative in all countries. The under-performance effect is not limited to developed countries, but also extends to emerging markets.

Thus, it appears that in most countries, IPO's underperform the market over periods of one to five years. While the initial underpricing of IPOs is confirmed internationally, the long-run performance results are mixed and further needs to be investigated.

There are several reasons why the long-run performance of initial public offerings is of interest. First, from an investor's viewpoint, the existence of price patterns

TABLE I

International Evidence on Long-run IPO Overpricing

Country	*Author(s)*	*Number of IPOs*	*Issuing years*	*Total abnormal return*
Australia	Lee, Taylor & Walter	266	1976-89	-46.50%
Austria	Aussenegg	57	1965-93	-27.30%
Brazil	Aggarwal, Leal & Hernandez	62	1980-90	-47.00%
Chile	Aggarwal, Leal & Hernandez	28	1982-90	-23.70%
Finland	Keloharju	79	1984-89	-21.10%
Germany	Ljungqvist	145	1970-90	-12.10%
Japan	Cai & Wei	172	1971-90	-27.00%
Korea	Kim, Krinsky & Lee	99	1985-88	2.00%
Singapore	Hin & Mahmood	45	1976-84	-9.20%
Sweden	Loughran, Ritter & Rydqvist	162	1980-90	1.20%
U.K.	Levis	712	1980-88	-8.10%
U.S.	Ritter (1991)	1526	1975-84	-29.1%
U.S.	Loughran & Ritter	4,753	1970-90	-20.00%

Note: Total abnormal returns are measured as 100*[(1+Ripo, T)/(1+Rm, T)] —100, where R IPO, T is the average total return on the IPOs from from the market price shortly after trading commences until the earlier of the delisting date or 3 years; Rm,T is the average of either the market return or matching-firm returns over the same interval.

Source: This is an updated version of Table 7 in Loughran, Ritter, and Rydqvist (1994).

may present opportunities for active trading strategies to produce superior returns. Second, a finding of non-zero aftermarket performance calls into question the informational efficiency of the IPO market. It provides evidence concerning Shiller's (1990) hypothesis that equity markets in general and the IPO market in particular are subject to fads that affect market prices. Third, the volume of IPOs displays large variations over time if the high volume periods are associated with poor long-run performance. This would indicate that issuers are successfully timing new issues to take advantage of "windows of opportunity". Fourth, the cost of external equity capital for companies going public depends not only upon the transaction costs incurred in going public but also upon the returns that investors receive in the after market. To the degree that low returns are earned in the aftermarket, the cost of external equity capital is lowered for these firms.

Long-run performance anomalies have become a growth area within the academic finance literature. They range from firm underperformance following mergers [Agarawal, Jaffe and Mandelker (1992)], dividend omissions [Michaely, Thaler, and Womack (1995)], exchange listing changes [Dharan and Ikenberry (1995)] and firm overperformance following share repurchases [Ikenberry, Lakonishok and Vermaelen (1995)]. In addition, Ritter (1991), Loughran and Ritter (1995), and Spiess and Affleck-Graves (1995) show that stock market performance subsequent to initial public offerings (IPOs) and seasoned equity offerings (SEOs) is poor. Both sets of authors explain underperformance in terms of investor sentiment: investors in SEOs and IPOs systematically underreact to the bad news conveyed in an equity issue.

To sum up, the international studies consistently find short-term underpricing. However, mixed results for long-term performance exist, with many countries showing underperformance. It is very confusing as to why IPO initial returns are significantly positive while long-run returns are negative. Typically, if all the investors expect that the long-run returns of IPO shares will be negative, through backward induction, no one will invest in IPOs in the initial markets. Therefore, the long-run underperformance of IPOs is an anomaly and needs further examining. Most of the studies reviewed above have been conducted abroad. The focus of these has been to measure the extent of underpricing in the short-run and overpricing in the long-run. These studies have attempted to examine the relationship among various variables like reputation of underwriter, auditor, etc. affecting the pricing of IPOs and pricing of IPOs. From research point of view, the area of IPOs has been a neglected aspect in India. There is a paucity of literature on IPOs in Indian context, especially in the regime following the abolition of CCI in 1992. Very little work has been done on the performance of IPOs in India. Only five or six studies have been conducted. Almost all these studies deal with only the short-run performance of new issues. Hence, need has been felt to further probe into the performance of IPOs in India. The present study is an attempt to examine the performance of Indian IPOs in terms of pricing.

Objectives of the Study

The main objective of the study is to evaluate the performance of IPOs in India during boom period. The specific objectives of the study is to carry out the analysis of performance in terms of return on IPOs for medium and long periods.

Period of the Study

The period chosen for the study is 1992 to 1996. This period has been chosen because Indian primary market experienced boom during this period. Moreover, it was during this period when a wave of liberalization started in the country, brought out structural changes in the Indian capital market. SEBI replaced CCI in the year 1992. It allowed free pricing of issues in June 1992. Following this, Indian primary market flourished like anything in 1993 and 1994. This boom continued till 1996. Thereafter, there was steep decline in the IPO market in terms of volume and value. It is generally believed that during this period (1992-96), many new companies approached the capital market and raised large resources on the basis of rosy projections and flimsy justifications. So, a need has been felt to examine the performance of these companies.

Universe of the study

The universe of the study consists of all the companies, which raised capital for the first time since their inception at par or premium and have been listed on BSE between June 1992 and December 31, 1996. The study has been restricted to the companies, which issued equity share capital during the period under study because it has been most favoured instrument for raising finance during this period. The companies, which used other instruments to raise funds, have been excluded from the universe.

Sample of the Study

The sample consists of 500 Indian companies which issued IPOs during June 1992-December 1996. Sample selection is based on the following criteria:

(1) The IPO is made in the free pricing era of SEBI.
(2) The IPO is listed on the BSE and has been traded for three years after listing. In other words, companies' pricing performance is available on the BSE for at least three years.
(3) Data regarding offer price, listing date, issue size, date of incorporation, appraisers and lead managers are available.

The sample selection is guided by the availability of data. The sample consists of 314 par issues and 186 premium issues. BSE Sensitive Index is selected as a representative of the market. BSE is selected, as it is the largest stock exchange of India. Almost 98% of the Indian companies are listed on BSE. Daily four values of Sensex are available viz. opening, high, low and closing value. We have taken closing value of the Sensex on different dates in order to calculate the market adjusted return. And in case the index is not available, a seven days window is selected and the nearest available date is selected. In order to analyse the after market performance, one week, one month, three months, six months, one year, two years and three years time intervals have been selected on the basis of studies conducted in other parts of the world. In case the share price is not available for a particular date, a seven days window has been considered for this and the price available on the nearest date has been selected

Measurement of Performance of IPOs

For the purpose of present study, following measures to examine the performance of IPOs have been used.

Aftermarket Price Performance

To evaluate long-term performance of Indian IPOs, long-term returns on the IPO price and the closing price on the first day of trading are calculated. These returns are measured by the difference in quotations at the end of 1 week, 1, 3, 6 months, 1, 2, 3 years and the initial price or the closing price on the first day of trading. These figures are compared with BSE Sensitive Index. Long-term returns are calculated without annualizing the data, dividing the difference between quotations and initial or closing prices on the first day of trading. When returns are adjusted to Sensex, the difference between the different quotations and the difference in index for both dates (from 1 week to 3 years) is calculated. The above discussion can be converted in. following formula:

$$R_{it} = \left[\left(P_{it}/P_{io}\right) - 1\right] \times 100$$

$$R_{mt} = \left[\left(P_{mt}/P_{mo}\right) - 1\right] \times 100$$

The average market adjusted returns on a portfolio of n stocks for event month t is the equally weighted arithmetic average of the market adjusted returns given by :

$$\text{Average } MAER_t = \frac{1}{n}\sum_{t=1}^{n} MAER_{it}$$

where

P_{it} = Price of the share of firm i at time t,
P_{io} = Offer price of share of the ith firm,
I_{mt} = Sensex at time t,
I_{mo} = Sensex on the offer day,
R_{it} = Raw return of firm i at time t, and
R_{mt} = Return on BSE Sensitive Index during period t.

To analyse the long-term performance, another measure Wealth Relative (Index) using the procedure employed by Ritter and Levis is calculated. The magnitude of this measure is an indication of the performance of IPOs *vis-a-vis* the market. A wealth relative greater than unity implies that IPOs outperformed the market in that period, while a wealth relative below 1 indicates under-performance. WR_{it} for a sample of n stocks from offer date, to date 't' is calculated using the formula:

$$\text{Wealth Relative } (WR_{it}) = \frac{1+\frac{1}{N}\sum_{i=1}^{n} r_{it}}{1+\frac{1}{N}\sum_{i=1}^{n} r_{mt}}$$

where

r_{it} = R_{it} /100,
r_{mt} = R_{mt} /100, and
N = total number of IPOs in the sample.

Statistical Techniques Used

In this section the various statistical techniques used to carry out the analysis is briefly described. All the statistical work has been done on SPSS/PC+ software.

One-Sample T-Test

The statistical significance of the average return (AR) is determined by using the usual t-statistic, which is computed for each period as:

$$t(AR) = AR_t/SE\ (AR_t)$$

where

$SE(AR_t)$ = standard error of the average return in period t, and
$t(AR_t)$ = t-statistic (with n-1 degrees of freedom) for the null hypothesis that the average return in any given period is zero.

Limitations of the Study

The present study is based on the secondary data collected from various sources mentioned earlier. Thus, the conclusions drawn are subject to the correctness of data. Some other limitations of the study are as follows:

- The IPOs considered in this study belong to the boom period. It would have been better if we had considered the IPOs in bear market (IPOs in 1997, 1998, 1999) to make a better comparison and draw better conclusions.

- Only equity shares have been considered in this study. Other instruments like preference shares could have been considered.
- Many structural changes have taken place in Indian capital market since 1996. The conclusions drawn may not be applicable to the present period.
- The results of the study are subject to the methods of measurement of returns and forecasting accuracy. The methods used to measure performance of IPOs in this study are those, which have been applied by other Indian studies. It would have been better if we had applied other methods such as Cumulative Adjusted Returns (CARs), Fama French Model, etc. in order to make results comparable with other international studies.
- BSE Sensitive Index (SENSEX) has been used for calculating MAERs. SENSEX is 30 scrips' index. It would have been better if we had used BSE 100, NIFTY, etc. and compared the results.

Sample Description

In this section, the characteristics of the sample selected for the study have been described. This information will be useful in analysing the performance of IPOs. The sample consists of 500 companies, which came to the market during 1992-96 and got listed on the Bombay Stock Exchange. Table 12.1 reports the distribution of IPOs by year of issuance and by issue size.

The largest number of IPOs is observed in 1994 with 235 IPOs, followed by 141 in 1995, 94 in 1993, 28 in 1996 and 2 IPOs in 1992. Furthermore, the highest percentage (62.31) of total proceeds is realized in 1995, followed by 25.61% in 1994, 8.33% in 1993, 3.68% in 1996 and 0.06% in 1992. In terms of number of IPOs, 1994 seems to be a dominant issue year and in terms of issue size, 1995 led others in Indian IPO market. Out of 500 IPOs, 314 firms issued shares at par and raised 21.76% of the total proceeds and 186 firms issued shares at premium and raised 78.24% of total issue size. These IPOs took minimum 42 days and maximum 761 days to list on the Bombay Stock Exchange. The average listing time is 99 days,

TABLE 2

Characteristics of the Sample

Year of Issuance	*Number of IPOs*	*Percentage out of Total*	*Issue Size*	*Percentage out of Total*
1992	2	00.40	385.80	00.06
1993	94	18.80	49926.91	08.33
1994	235	47.00	153556.21	25.61
1995	141	28.20	373573.45	62.31
1996	28	05.60	22061.50	03.68
Total	500	100.00	599503.87	100.00
Par Issues	314	62.80	130465.02	21.76
Premium Issues	186	37.20	469038.85	78.24

much higher than SEBI's requirement. Out of these 500 IPOs, 324 belong to manufacturing sector, 119 to service sector, 9 to mining and drilling sector and 48 to miscellaneous sector. Further, 316 IPOs are listed in 1994, followed by 117 in 1995, 59 in 1996 and 8 in 1993. As far as lead managers are concerned, SBI Caps handled the maximum number of IPOs in the sample and 41 lead managers handled one issue each in the years under study. The minimum age of the sample is 166 days and maximum age of the sample is 115 years. The average age of the sample is 8.61 years. Other characteristics of the sample have been given and discussed alongwith the analysis of performance of IPOs.

Long Run Performance of IPOs in India

In this section, an effort has been made to study the long-run performance of Indian IPOs using various measures such as mean raw return, MAER, mean annualized raw as well as market adjusted returns and wealth relatives. Due to underpricing, the high returns on the first day make it advisable to calculate long-term returns on the IPO price (i.e. including initial returns) and the closing price on the first day of trading (excluding initial returns). These returns have been measured by the difference in quotations at the end of 1 week, 1 month, 3 months, 6 months, 1 year, 2 years and 3 years and the initial price or the listing price. As discussed in

TABLE 3

Overall Returns Given by Indian IPOs (Including Initial Returns)

	Wealth Index	*Average*			
		Raw Returns	*MAERs*	*Annualised Raw Returns*	*Annualised MAERs*
Listing day	1.70	83.22*	75.16*	353.47*	331.13*
One Week after Listing	1.72	85.43*	77.33*	332.03*	311.06*
One Month after Listing	1.68	81.55*	73.23*	251.34*	233.38*
Three Months after Listing	1.76	90.72*	82.65*	185.11*	172.70*
Six Months after Listing	1.89	101.22*	94.48*	134.23*	127.51*
One Year after Listing	1.56	54.70*	55.37*	42.69*	43.92*
Two Years after Listing	0.81	(-) 19.29*	(-) 19.33*	(-) 8.78*	(-) 8.63*
Three Years after Listing	0.52	(-) 42.50*	(-) 52.98*	(-) 13.06*	(-) 16.19*

* Significantly different from zero at 1 percent level.

chapter 3, the evidence on long-term returns of IPOs all over the world is not conclusive. That is why this aspect of IPO performance has been probed in the following paragraphs.

The overall returns calculated from offer price are given in Table 3.

All the returns, positive or negative, are significantly different from zero. The raw returns, which are 83.22% on listing day, went up to 101.22% at the end of six months and then went down sharply, though remained positive, at the end of one year. Thereafter, these returns became negative at the end of second and third year.

The annualized raw as well as MAER have declined consistently over the entire period. These remained positive up to one year and then became negative in the second and third year. When the value of wealth index and MAER are compared over the period, the results are found to be same as those for raw returns. Simply stating, if investors in India were allocated with new issues at the offer price during 1992-96 and they held them for six months, they would have earned 101.22% on their investments. If they held shares up to one year, their returns would be lesser but positive. However, if they held shares for two years, the returns would reduce to (-) 19.29% and further reduce to (-) 42.50% at the end of third year.

When the returns are calculated on the basis of closing price on the first trading day, these drop considerably due to the first day underpricing [See Table 3(a)]. In other words, the investors who purchased the issue in the after market at the closing price on first trading day and held for one week, received mean raw and market adjusted returns of 3.62% and 3.61% respectively. These returns continue to be positive in the increasing order in the first, third and six months and then drop out considerably and become negative till the end of third year. The wealth relative is more than one up to six months and thereafter becomes less than one up to third year.

Thus, long-run performance tends to decline with increasing holding periods. This is true independent of the fact as to whether the shares are bought on the primary or on secondary market.

The present findings appear to confirm that long-run performance of IPOs in India is the same as in other countries. In other words, IPOs are good short-term investment opportunity (up to one year), becoming non-profitable as of two years, with under-performance increasing as of third year.

TABLE 3(a)

Overall Returns Given by Indian IPOs (Excluding Initial Returns)

Period	*Wealth Index*	*Raw Returns*	*MAER*
One Week after Listing	1.04	3.62*	3.61*
One Month after Listing	1.02	1.88	1.61
Three Months after Listing	1.08	8.50*	8.30*
Six Months after Listing	1.17	15.09*	16.52*
One Year after Listing	0.96	-10.87*	-3.33
Two Years after Listing	0.53	-49.95*	-43.60*
Three Years after Listing	0.37	-61.12*	-65.53*

* Significantly different from zero at 1 percent level.

TABLE 4

Returns Given by Indian IPOs: Par and Premium Issues (Including Initial Return)

Period	Par Issues (314)					Premium Issues (186)				
	Wealth Index	Raw Returns	MAER	Annual-ised Raw Returns	Annual-ised MAER	Wealth Index	Raw Returns	MAER	Annual-ised Raw Returns	Annual-ised MAER
Listing day	1.79	96.56*	86.49*	405.35*	377.62*	1.54	60.70*	56.02*	265.89*	252.64*
One Week after Listing	1.85	103.47*	93.20*	399.06*	372.24*	1.48	54.99*	50.54*	218.86*	207.79*
One Month after Listing	1.81	100.14*	89.56*	307.72*	284.30*	1.44	50.17*	45.66*	156.17*	147.42*
Three Months after Listing	1.92	113.68*	102.63*	231.74*	213.99*	1.47	51.97*	48.91*	106.39*	103.00*
Six Months after Listing	2.10	128.73*	119.69*	170.94*	161.47*	1.50	54.77*	51.91*	72.26*	70.17*
One Year after Listing	1.73	73.36*	73.01*	57.49*	57.96*	1.26	23.21**	25.58**	17.72***	20.20**
Two Years after Listing	0.88	(-) 10.71***	(-) 11.99***	(-) 4.90***	(-) 5.26***	0.68	(-) 33.78*	(-) 31.72*	(-) 15.35*	(-) 14.32*
Three Years after Listing	0.57	(-) 34.83*	(-) 49.11*	(-) 10.68*	(-) 14.95*	0.43	(-) 55.44*	(-) 59.51*	(-) 17.08*	(-) 18.29*

* Significantly different from zero at 1 percent level.
** Significantly different from zero at 5 percent level.
*** Significantly different from zero at 10 percent level.

Long-run Performance of Par and Premium Issues

The hypothesis that par issues have better prospects for future than premium issues has been tested to find out whether any significant differences exist. Table 4 reveals that par issues are far better than premium issues in terms of after market price performance up to a year ahead.

Beyond that both gave negative returns. The returns given by par and premium issues are significantly different from zero. The par issues gave significantly higher returns compared to the overall sample and premium issues gave significantly lower returns than the overall sample for all the time intervals for which the returns were calculated. In case of par issues, the raw returns and MAER show increasing trend up to six months and then decreasing trend up to three years. But when annualized raw returns and MAERs are considered, both show consistently decreasing trends. In case of premium issues, all the measures of returns show decreasing trend. The wealth relative shows that both type of issues overperformed the market up to one year and thereafter underperformed the market.

Table 4(a) reveals the performance of both types of issues excluding initial return.

TABLE 4(a)

Returns Given by Indian IPOs: Par and Premium Issues (Excluding Initial Return)

Period	*Par Issues (314)*			*Premium Issues (186)*		
	Wealth Index	*Raw Returns*	*MAER*	*Wealth Index*	*Raw Returns*	*MAER*
One Week after Listing	1.05	4.88*	4.70*	1.02	1.49	1.77
One Month after Listing	1.03	3.86	3.24	0.99	-1.46	-1.14
Three Months after Listing	1.13	14.14*	12.89*	1.01	-1.02	0.55
Six Months after Listing	1.26	24.72*	25.68*	1.01	-1.18	1.05
One Year after Listing	1.05	-3.86	4.32	0.83	-22.70*	-16.25*
Two Years after Listing	0.58	-46.25*	-39.53*	0.46	-56.19*	-50.48*
Three Years after Listing	0.40	-57.50*	-64.20*	0.33	-67.23*	-67.76*

* Significantly different from zero at 1 percent level.

In case of par issues, the raw returns are positive up to

a period of six months and MAERs are positive up to one year; thereafter both are negative. In case of premium issues, the raw returns are positive for one week only. The MAERs are positive for one week, 3 months and 6 months time intervals only. It clearly shows that par issues give better long-term returns than premium issues.

From the above discussion, it is clear that premium issues fared badly in the short-run and very badly in the long-run. Short-run underpricing is not sustained for long and the issues became overpriced. Premium issues have benefited the issuers but it has shattered the confidence of long-term investors

Long-run performance of Indian companies is also in line with what has been observed in other countries. Returns in the Indian market continue to be good for up to one year, but the situation changes in second and third year and returns become negative. In other words, IPOs are good short-term investment opportunity (up to one year), becoming unprofitable as of two years with underperformance increasing as of third year. A strategy of investing in IPOs at the end of first day of public trading and holding them for three years would have left the investors with only 52 paise relative to each rupee from investing in a group of companies forming Sensex, listed on BSE. It indicates that buying an IPO on offer date/listing date and holding for long-term period is not a better option as compared to the selling IPO in the initial days of secondary market trading. The various cross-sectional and time series pattern in long-run performance of IPOs are presented below:

(1) The raw and MAERs from offer date remains positive up to one year and becomes negative in 2nd and 3rd years. But if we calculate, returns from listing date (excluding initial return), these decline steeply but remains positive up to a period of six months only and then becomes negative.

(2) Par issues are far better than premium issues in terms of after market price performance up to a year ahead. Beyond that both give negative returns. Premium issues fared badly in the short-run and very badly in the long-run. As the amount of

premium increases, the amount of returns declines in almost all the time intervals. Premium issues have benefitted the issuers, but it has shattered the confidence of long-term investors.

Thus, it can be concluded that Indian IPOs overperform market in the short-run and underperform the market in the long-run.

On the whole, Indian IPO market is characterized by pervasive underpricing in the short-run and underperformance in the long-run. Indian investors have got very good returns up to a period of six months and thereafter the returns have declined. The long-term investors who continued to hold their investments for a period of 2-3 years have experienced negative returns. Further, majority of the companies, which approached the market during 1992-96 boom, could not achieve their projections. This fact confirms the general belief that the companies mispriced their issues on the basis of rosy projections. The findings have put a question mark on the reliability of projections in the prospectuses.

References

Agarawal, A., Jaffe, J. and Mandelker, G. (1992), "The post-merger performance of acquiring firms: A re-examination of an anomaly", *Journal of Finance*, 47, 1605-21.

Dharan, B. and Ikenberry, D. (1995), "The long-run negative drift of post-listing stock returns", *Journal of Finance*, 50, 1547-74.

Ikenberry, D., Lakonishok, J. and Vermaelen, T. (1995), "Market underreaction to open market share repurchases", *Journal of Financial Economics*, 39, 181-208.

Loughran, T., Ritter, J. and Rydqvist, K. (1994), "Initial public offerings: International insights", *Pacific-Basin Finance Journal*, 2, 165-99.

Loughran, Tim and Ritter, Jay R. (1995), "The New Issues Puzzle", *Journal of Finance*, 50(1), 23-51.

Michaely, R., Thaler, R. and Womack, K. (1995), "Price reactions to dividend initiations and omissions", *Journal of Finance*, 38, 1597-1606.

Ritter, J.R. (1991), "The long-run performance of initial public offerings", *Journal of Finance*, 46(1), 3-28.

Shiller, R.J. (1990), "Speculative prices and popular models", *Journal of Economic Perspectives*, 4, 55-65.

Spiess, K., Affleck-Graves, J. (1995), "The long-run performance following seasoned equity issues", *Journal of Financial Economics*, 38, 243-67.

Stoll, Hans R. and Curley, Anthony J. (1970), "Small Business and the New Issues Market for Equities", *Journal of Financial and Quantitative Analysis*, 5(3), 309-22.

Index